THE STORY OF
GOD'S LOVE AND POWER

JOHN MARINELLI

PREFACE

This is a fictional story, but the message it tells is real. It is all about God's love and healing power that is expressed in a wild horse and a Christian grandma. I chose this title because it reflected the interaction of people, situations, and hardships falling like dominos, under the mighty power of God as he answered a little girl's prayer.

The book will address such matters as:

- Does God love every human being?
- Is prayer relevant for today?
- Is divine healing possible in a world of science?
- Does God use animals to bless people?
- Does everyone have a divine destiny?
- Can a person's destiny change?
- Is it ok to commit suicide?
- Is God ok with abortion?
- Does God allow free will?
- Must a person be born again?
- And much more.

The storyline is about a thirteen-year-old girl named Jessie who lost her father in WWII and struggles with a low self-image. She is walking down a road that will destroy her dreams and crush her inward hopes of ever being a real person.

As the story unfolds, the reader will see Jessie become a rebel being, self-absorbed, cynical, and angry at life. However, the reader will also see the hand of God reaching down from heaven to comfort her and give her a sense of acceptance through her Christian grandma and a horse that shows up on her grandmother's farm in Iowa as fall turns into winter.

As in most of the author's books, there is a gallery of inspirational Christian Poetry for the benefit of those who enjoy thought-provoking poems.

INTRODUCTION

Our story begins with the "Shotgun" wedding of Tom Rowen and Mary Howard. The year was 1944. It was near the end of WWII. Tom and Mary were childhood sweethearts who went too far on a date when Tom was home on leave from the Army.

Mary's mother coined the phrase, "Shotgun Wedding" because Mary's dad insists that the two lovers get married or he would, well, you know what I mean.

"Too Far" were the words their parents used to describe Mary's teenage pregnancy. Mary said she loved Tom and just had to be with him. She says, "You never know what will happen."

Well, Mary's worst nightmare came true. Tom was in the Army Air Corps. Enemy fire brought down Tom's plane during daytime bombing raids over Germany. Tom's plane was one of 15 that did not make it back that day.

A few days later, Army officials informed Mary that her husband, whom she had married sixteen weeks before, was missing in action and presumed dead. There she was with a baby on the way and parents that were anxious about her being a teen mother and widower, all alone to face an uncertain world.

Tom and Mary, as most newlyweds do, tossed around

names for a child for when the time comes. Mary liked Jessie, after her great aunt, but Tom hoped for a boy and wanted to call him Butch.

They did not know that Mary was pregnant when Tom was home on leave. Mary wrote to Tom in a letter about her situation, but he never had the chance to read it. Before the letter arrived, the military declared Tom killed in action and returned Mary's letter unopened, along with his personal effects.

So life went on as it did for thousands of folks caught up in war, economic struggles, and heartaches. Mary gave birth to a beautiful baby girl named Jessie, as she had planned when Tom was alive.

The war ended and Jessie became the center of attention in family life, with everyone spoiling her and giving her everything she wanted. As Jessie grew up, she became increasingly bitter and angry at God because her friends had fathers and she was all alone in a single-parent home, where her mother had to work two jobs to make ends meet. She felt she was missing the family life that other kids took for granted.

As Jessie approached her teen years, she rebelled against society, religion, school, and any other establishment that might try to tell her what to do or how to be. She sought others who were in rebellion, joined a neighborhood gang, and started using illegal drugs. She was on the "Fast Track" to nowhere and nobody seemed to care.

Jessie's mother, Mary, stayed single. She never remarried or even dated. She lived in a world of heartache fashioned from sorrow and sadness because of the loss of Tom, her first and only love.

13 years have passed since Tom's death, and life was not going anywhere until Mary got a phone call from her mother, Jessie's grandma, who lived in Iowa. Grandpa Joe had just passed away at 87 and Grandma Elizabeth was afraid to live alone on their 40-acre farm. She needed help to keep the 100-year homestead in the family.

It was like a call from heaven to Mary that answered her prayers. She knew life could not go on as it had been. Jessie needed help and so did she. Grandma's invitation to move to Iowa was a chance to start over, and she took it.

CHAPTER ONE:
GROWING UP IN A TROUBLED WORLD

J ESSIE'S ANGER AND BITTERNESS TOWARDS God and society were also in Mary's heart. They both felt the heartache of losing a loved one. Jessie yearned for someone she never knew, while Mary mourned the sudden loss of her only true love. Both blamed God for letting this happen. Mary kept her anger hidden in her heart so no one could see. But Jessie expressed her misery everywhere she went and to everyone she met.

They were two broken hearts in a troubled world searching for something they knew not what. Mary protected her heart by staying single so she would not have to face such a loss again while Jessie vocalized her self-imposed torment through actions of rebellion. Both had concluded that it was God's fault.

The following week, there was a special report on T.V. about gang violence. Police interviews identified three gang members from Jessie's neighborhood. Two gang members lost their lives in a shootout over turf rights, and another gang member was on the verge of death. They did not expect the surviving gang member, who suffered severe injuries, to recover.

This turf war ended Jessie's involvement in gangs and drugs. She hid from any appearance of being a gang member for fear of being arrested and serving time in jail for her participation in the gang's illegal activities.

Before the gang war, Jessie would never have agreed to moving to Iowa, but now she felt it was her escape from prosecution. Apart from the boy who suffered severe injuries in the gang war, she had no real friends. She had no real interests outside of illegal activities and juvenile pranks.

Despite knowing that life would be different in Iowa, she had her attitude and anger to protect her. She figured she could dominate and even bully if necessary to keep herself safe from the unknown.

Mary and Jessie were living in a 2-bedroom rental apartment in Miami, Florida. Mary thought it would help Jessie if she had a dog, so they went to the animal shelter and Jessie picked out a mut. The aid said it was a Heins-57 variety. Jessie immediately called the male dog, "Meatball."

Mary was confused. She says, "Why on earth do you want to call this little dog, "Meatball?"

Jessie replies, "because I like meatballs and spaghetti. I think it will be fun to say, come here, Meatball. Plus, I like to be different."

So they brought "Meatball" home to their little apartment. He was just a pup, only 16 weeks old. He had to be trained, housebroken, and taught to come when called.

Mary says to Jessie, "It is your dog. You will have to take care of it, which means walking him to do his business, playing with him so he does not get bored, teaching him to obey and feeding him twice a day."

Jessie agrees. Mary thought to herself, "How can the rebellious teach the rebellious?"

Before the gang wars, Jessie ran with the crowd. She was into everything illegal, from stealing hubcaps with the guys to beating up old folks and taking their money. She even went along as a lookout for the gang as they robbed a convenience store. There was nothing she would not do to keep her tough-girl status. When she attended school, her attitude often resulted in her being sent to the principal's office or detention.

Jessie never went to church or even read the Bible. Those things were part of the establishment, and she was rebelling against them. Morality, righteousness, and being good were not in her vocabulary. Alcohol, sex, drugs, and anything else that could take her away from being happy ruled her spirit.

Jessie often hung out with Tommy. He was the gang member that was not expected to live. He sustained severe injuries in the last gang war encounter. She chose Tommy because he had the same name as her father. She somehow felt that being with him would bring back her dad, but this Tom was a hoodlum, whereas her dad was a hero. There was a big difference, but not in Jessie's emotions. She craved affection and a relationship and was willing to be with anyone to get it. She never realized that her rebellion against the establishment was, in fact, a slap in the face to her dad, who served the establishment and gave his life to defend it.

Well, evil Tommy and confused Jessie ran together as "Bro & Bitch," names given to them by the gang. Both "Bro & Bitch" were growing up in a troubled world. They both hated society and religion. Their position was, "it's better to be an atheist than a two-faced phony."

Mary knew Jessie was out of control and twice threatens her with juvenile court orders for detention in a reform school. But Jessie did not care. She knew the gang would hide her and protect her because that was what they did when one member got in trouble. Mary was at her wits' end. For the first time in years, she called out to God. This was just before Grandma called. God had answered her with a telephone call from Springville, Iowa.

Post WWII was hard on single moms. The returning GIs needed jobs and women were once again moved back to their "Stay At Home" status. The nearly overwhelming economic pressures and troubled home environment were almost too much for Mary to handle.

When WWII officially ended in 1945, Americans celebrated the end of rationing, and they ushered in a new era of hope. America saw major changes occurring in the roles of females. Many argued that the woman's place was in the home with the children, while others disagreed with this mindset.

After years of economic depression followed by war, many Americans were ready to get married and start families. Post-war America saw a baby boom. 1940s, America saw incredibly high birth rates. 1946 saw the highest rate of births ever, with 3.4 million births, and the rate continued to climb in the following years. From 1954 to 1964, over 4 million babies were born each year.

As the baby boom erupted, so did the development of suburbs that offered housing for families. There were also changes in music, with the addition of rock and roll. Segregation led to many protests and events to encourage equality. Things were changing in the American society and it was a difficult time for a lot of folks.

The following thirteen years were full of hardship and sorrow. Mary had a difficult time making ends meet, and Jessie had to take care of herself. She became a victim of the turmoil and gave in to the same passions that her mother felt during pre-war times. She was pregnant and mom did not like it at all. All-the-more reason to move in with Grandma.

"Hello," Grandma answers. "Hi mother, It's me", says Mary. "I have some news for you that might keep us from moving in with you on the farm.

"Oh, What's up;" says Grandma.

"Well, I guess I will just say it. Jessie is pregnant." Replied Mary.

"Oh no," says Grandma. "How did this happen?"

Mary, "It was not the stork. It was her gang member boyfriend. Now what do I do?"

"You do the same thing I did when you turned up pregnant", says Grandma. "You cry a lot. You pray a lot. Sacrificing your life and future is how you ensure your child can have hers." "That is what I did."

Mary, "Or, I can talk her into having an abortion. That will help her and me. That will take all the stress and worry off both of us."

"What are you, crazy?" says Grandma. "You are suggesting an action that will end the life of your grandchild and my great grandchild. How can you tell your child to murder her unborn baby?"

"They say that in the early stages, it's just a blob and not really living." Said Mary.

"You don't believe that, do you, Mary?" says Grandma. "God help you if you take this child's life. You will be guilty of murder, which God said in his 10-commandments, "thou shalt not kill."

"Did you know they can detect a heartbeat in the fetus between 10 and 13 weeks?" Said Grandma. "It is not a blob. It is a new life being formed by God,"

"Well, I would have to take her to California where abortion is legal or go to a back street hack that might endanger her life, said Mary…so I'll forget that idea for now."

Well, grandma ended her phone conversation with Mary in an attitude of praise and thanksgiving to God for her answered prayers. She always hoped that Mary would find a life and be happy. She believed that her faith would make a difference and seeing the hand of God answering her prayers for Mary brought her great joy. Soon, the three girls, Jessie, Mary, and Grandma, would be together and life would slow down for all of them. They could talk about problems and deal with issues as a family.

However, there were other more pressing issues looming over Mary that demanded her undivided attention before she moved to Iowa. Jessie was out of control. She fought with her mother almost around the clock. Oh, it did not matter why or about what. They just screamed at each other and said every curse word they could think of.

Jessie's attitude was driving Mary crazy. She just would not give in to anything that was helpful. Mary felt deeply troubled and had thoughts of suicide. The last few years were so bad that Mary hated her own daughter and wished she had never given birth to her.

The seed of despair that grew in Mary's heart when she lost Tom was larger than life. It had not only taken over Mary's soul, but slowly spread to Jessie. The future was bleak at best. Mary started looking for a way to get out of the pain she felt, but there was no clear path to peace of mind. That nagging thought of ending her own life grew bigger with each argument.

Jessie, "Dear diary…I hate fighting with my mother but I cannot let her get the better of me. She just does not understand."

Mary contemplated ending her life every day. Life became unbearable for her. She even mentally put together a suicide note but never actually wrote it down. She often tells herself, "It will soon be over and I will be free."

Back then, people did not openly discuss suicide. Mary got caught in its web. The big question was, "How to do it?" Does she use a gun, knife, rope, overdose, fumes from her car or what? Back in the 1950s, firearms and explosives were more frequently used for committing suicide than any other means of injury. This category, composed principally of deaths attributed to self-inflicted gunshot wounds, accounted for 48 percent of all suicides. Hanging and strangulation were the next most frequent means and accounted for about 15 percent of the total suicides. About 12 percent were from poisoning by analgesic and soporific substances. The only other category which accounted for over 10 percent of the suicides was poisoning by other gases. (United States Division of Vital Statistics)

Mary was about to become among the 1% of all deaths in the United States caused by suicide, which still ranked in the top 10 causes of death today. Late one night, while Jessie was asleep, Mary began to mentally plan her death. She took pencil and paper and jotted down when and where her life would end. Then she wrote a note to Jessie telling her why she was killing herself.

The note listed four things that Mary felt justified her committing suicide. I know what Mary said because I found the note. It said:

- God does not love me anymore, that is why.

- Your birth and rebellious life have destroyed mine.

- Because of what I did to Suzie when you were born.

- I have no hope and nothing to live for.

Mary included in her suicide note the location where Jessie could find her body. She placed the note on the mantle in a sealed envelope with Jessie's name on it. Then she took her army issued pistol with ammo and placed it on her nightstand. She had kept Tom's pistol for all those years, just for such a time as this.

I was concerned about Mary's despondency and called on the phone about 9 PM, but there was no answer. After five calls over an hour, I dropped by to check on Mary. I was privileged to have an extra key in case Mary needed it, so I let myself in.

The apartment appeared disheveled and messy. Jessie was not at home and the T.V. was on the Syfy channel. As I looked around, I noticed the note on the mantle. I opened it, read it, and immediately called 911.

I just could not believe that Mary would want to take her own life. I gave the police the location where Mary said her body would be and then I jumped in my car and sped away to the location Mary gave. It was about a 20- minute drive.

I arrived shortly after the police to find Mary sitting on a park bench with powder burns on her face and hands. She did what she said she was going to do, but the ammo from WWII was old and the bullet casing exploded, spewing gun powder all over Mary. She suffered minor powder burns.

I rushed over to her and held her for a long while until she stopped crying. I gave the suicide note to the police and told them she had been suicidal for a long time. Then the police arrested her for trying to kill herself. It was illegal to attempt suicide. She would now have to be evaluated by county hospital doctors and appear in court to determine if she was at risk for another suicide attempt.

I went back to Mary's apartment to be with Jessie, but she was not there. I cleaned up a bit and waited. She finally came home with a boyfriend around 4-AM. The tattooed guy was not her beloved. He was still in the hospital. This guy was a real druggie, hard and mean looking. They were both surprised to see me.

Jessie, "Who are you? And why are you here?

I asked the guy to leave, as I needed to talk to Jamet about personal family issues. The guy mumbled something as he left. Then I asked Jessie to sit down, and I told her about what happened to her mother and where she was.

Jessie read the suicide note and was angry. She says, "So I am to blame for my mother's attempted suicide. What did I ever do to her? I did not ask to be born. It just happened. Maybe I should kill myself and end her misery. She never loved me anyway."

Jessie, Dear diary, "Am I so worthless that no one wants me? I will probably end up in a foster home. Thanks Mom."

I told Jessie that I was a social worker and her mother will not be going ahead with the move to Iowa. I said that she will be in the hospital for a long while because she is irrational, despondent, and deeply depressed.

I exaggerated Mary's condition, but Jessie bought it. I had my reasons. Mary was just where I wanted her, and I had Jessie. I planned this for years and my plan was working.

Jessie, Dear diary, "Maybe I should run away and live on the streets. Living here is just too hard."

CHAPTER TWO
THE BIG DECEPTION

THE NEXT DAY, I TOLD Jessie who I really was. She thought I was a social worker from the juvenile court. I asked her to sit down, and I said, "Jessie, you will not believe this, but it is true."

She says, "Not going to believe what?"

I replies, "I am Suzie, your birth mother. Mary stole you from me just after you were born."

Jessie, "Mary is my mother. You are a Liar."

"No," I replies, "Mary is my twin sister. In fact, we are identical twins."

Jessie, "You don't look like her."

Suzie, "I almost do. When I dye my hair, put on her clothes, and adjust my accent, you will not be able to tell the difference. Remember, it has been many years since we were together."

Jessie, "Where have you been all these years? Why didn't you try to get me back? Why did you abandon me?

Suzie, your grandma forced me to leave when I got pregnant. She hated me for what I did."

Jessie, "And what did you do that was so bad?

Suzie, "Tom and Jessie were just married. Mary told your grandma she was pregnant so she could marry Tom, but she was not pregnant. I was." However, "No one knew it, including me."

Here is what happened. "The night before Tom was to report to his army base, I acted like I was Mary and went into Tom before Mary came home from shopping. We laid together for an hour. Then I slipped away before Mary returned. Remember, then, we were look alike sisters. It was easy to be Mary and I could do it and did it and I got pregnant by Tom. He never knew it was me. I told Mary what happened, and she kept quiet, except for telling Grandma after Tom left for the Army."

Jessie, "Why did you do that?"

Suzie, "Because I hated Mary. She took Tom away from me. I had the 1st date with Tom. I was the 1st one who kissed him and I wanted to be the 1st one to make love to him. She jumped in, acting as if she were me, and stole his heart. Then she told him she was Mary and not me. By then, Tom did not care because we were identical twins. He felt to have Mary was to have me and they were well on their way to a serious relationship."

Jessie, "She tricked you back then and now you are getting back at her, right?"

Suzie, "Right! I decided I will be Mary, once again, and get back my daughter, that is you, who was taken from me without my consent."

Jessie, Dear Diary… "Wow, this is heavy. I do not know what to think."

Suzie, "Of course, if you would rather stay with Mary, I will back off. But, if you want your actual mother, me, I am here. But because Suzie vanished years ago, I will have to be Mary."

Jessie, "What about Mary and Grandma?"

Suzie, "With your help, I can fool your grandma. You just need to bring me up to date with what has happened. Mary is in a place for the insane. My sources tell me her court case did not go well. The authorities scheduled her for a 1-5-year treatment plan. I heard she tried to kill herself again while in that place. She will pay for what she did to me."

Jessie," how did you just disappear?"

Suzie, "I faked my death by drowning. I was swimming in the ocean and got into a riptide. It pulled me out to sea. I was an excellent swimmer and could get free, but it looked like I had drowned to those on the beach. I played it up and screamed for help so the lifeguard noticed me but he could not get to me. The currents were too rough. I swam down the beach away from the crowd and came to shore. Then I grabbed my stuff and left the city.

Jessie, "How do I know you are telling the truth? I have never heard your name spoken or even seen pictures of you."

Suzie, "I thought you would want to see some proof, so I made copies of a few legal documents. Here is my birth certificate. See, it shows your grandma as my birth mother. Here are some photos that did not get destroyed because I hid them. See the two little girls? They are identical twins. That is Mary and myself at 5-years old.

Jessie, "So, what's in it for me if I go along with this scam?"

Suzie, "Money! I plan to make grandma pay for her rejection of me all those years. When I am through, she will sign over the deed to her farm and we will sell it and split the profits. It could exceed $100,000 each. Remember, she was in cahoots with Mary to deceive you and hide my existence. She never loved you and always complained to Mary about you.

Jessie, "Ok, I will play along for now, because the police are after me and I need a place to hide."

Suzie, "well, a farm in Iowa is the perfect place. You can have a new beginning. No one will know about your past. You can reinvent yourself. We will be nice and helpful for a while until Grandma turns over the deed, but then we will throw her out on her ear. Just remember to keep calling me Mom. I am really your mom, you know. As far as Suzie, she no longer exists."

Jessie, "Ok" Dear Diary…" This seems like a bad dream. I cannot believe it is all happening to me."

So Jessie and the new Mary packed up their belonging and proceeded to grandma's house. Meanwhile, the wolf was begging at their door. The police got wind of Jessie's plans to run and were surveilling the little apartment, waiting for her to return. There was a bench warrant for her arrest over a matter of theft and other criminal activities.

Before departing, Jessie saw a gang member in a restaurant who told her the police were after her, big time. That stopped them from going back to the apartment. They headed straight for Iowa.

Jessie, Dear diary…" I wonder if my real mom is real or is she an evil person trying to hurt my real mom? I am afraid but feel sad for the Mary back in Miami."

Once we were on the road, we stopped at a rest area so I could call grandma. I had all Mary's identification and important phone numbers. I had died my hair, put on Mary's clothes, and now looked just like her.

Suzie, "Hello grandma, this is Mary." "I am with Jessie. We are on the road to your place. We just left, so it will be a day or so before we get there."

Grandma, "Good, I am so happy that you are coming. I have the rooms ready and will make a fresh apple pie to celebrate your safe arrival. I have been praying and believe that God will be with you all the way."

Suzie, "God has too much on his plate to worry about us. We will do just fine on our own."

Grandma, "Oh, it will not be any trouble. God always hears my prayers and is attentive to my plea. He is on our side, remember? Well, I should say we are on his side." He will send his angels to protect us and his Holy Spirit to guide us. The Bible even says, "The angel of the Lord encamps around about them that fear (Reverence) him, to deliver them." Psalm 34:7.

Suzie, "So if I do not fear God, he will not protect me? That is not fair. I do not think I like your God anymore."

Grandma, "Fear means reverence. "We were created to love and worship God. That is our destiny. You know that, Mary. You learned all about it in Sunday school. Why wouldn't you trust him now? We will talk more about it when you get here. Lord, give them a safe trip."

Jessie, "Hi grandma, I have a lot of things I want to

say about God and growing up. I blame God for most of my faults. I want to hear what you have to say."

Grandma, "Ok honey. We will talk, if you want, about any subject."

Suzie, "We got to get back on the road. I will check in later tonight."

Suzie, "So we got back on the road and I opened a conversation with Jessie. Why are you going to talk to your grandma about God? She is a religious fanatic. She will surely lead you away from being yourself."

Jessie, "I do not care. I want to hear what she has to say." There must be a reason she thinks as she does. I want to know why.

Suzie, "Ok, but remember, I told you the truth. She will distort the truth and confuse you as to what life is all about."

Jessie, "Ok smarty-pants, what is life all about?

Suzie, "It's not about being a puppet for a mysterious, unknowable god." Life, as I see it, is being your own god. You are the master of your own destiny and can make it what you want it to be. There are no rules and regulations except what you want. People are fools and you can rule over them and manipulate them into doing your will. The idea of God just gets in the way."

Jessie, "So, if everyone thought like you, we would all be gods fighting over weak-minded folks we can deceive. That sounds to me like all chiefs and no Indians."

Suzie, "Listen, life is what you say it is. You cannot allow someone else to tell you otherwise. If you do, they will take away your identity and cause you to be like what they think is proper. You should decide those matters for yourself."

Jessie, "But, what if there is a God? What will we do when he calls us after we die? I do not think I should dismiss the notion until I investigate it further."

Suzie, "You know what? I believe when we die, that is it. We are gone, nonexistent. That is why I eat, drink and be happy all the time. I am doing things that please me because, when I die, everything ends."

Jessie, "If that is true, why do anything? Everything we do has no purpose. Life is not worth living because it has no meaning except to occupy our time until we die. That makes little or no sense. I must have more value than that. There must be a reason I am alive. Why am I here? If there is a God, what does he want from me? Where will I spend eternity? Is there a heaven and a hell? I need to know these things."

Suzie, "Do you honestly think that your grandma can answer these questions? Everyone wants to know, but there is no rule of thumb or book you can read to find the answers. We all make it up as we go along. That is what I do, and it is working for me."

Jessie, "Grandma quoted from her Bible. Maybe that is the book that has all the answers."

So Susie, that is me playing the role of Mary, Jessie's mother, and Jessie, being her troubled self, drove on towards their new life on grandma's Iowa farm.

"Wait a minute," says Jessie. "I think it is about time that I continue this story. You have said enough."

I felt troubled because I had experienced rejection

and grew up without a father. I was living a life of crime and ran with the bad boys. I sold my soul for acceptance and love. It was time to start over and find my true self without all the attitudes and fear. My hate for grandma was weakening the closer we got to the farm."

Janer, Dear Diary…" I feel anxious about grandma and farming. I hope I can deal with it."

CHAPTER THREE
LIFE AND LIBERTY IN IOWA

J ESSIE CONTINUES, "MY WORLD WAS about to change, and I did not know just how much. Miami was full of tall buildings and lots of people running around feverishly in search of money, power, and fame. I had to be "street smart" to survive. I called Miami, "the little big city on the bay" because I lived close to Biscayne Bay and it was one of the fastest growing cities in the country. There were lots of stores, some fantastic parks, of course, the beaches and lots to do. An out-of-control teenage girl could get lost easily, and I did just that, got lost in the shuffle."

"Iowa was nothing like Miami. Instead of sprawling population growth, there were rolling hills and fields that were full of things that grow in the rich Iowa soil. You could drive for miles and see nothing else but corn fields, cows, and big red barns. The population of Springville was around 750 folks opposed to 250,000 in Miami."

"Springville was about 14 miles from Cedar Rapids. Now that was a city. It had nice department stores, a museum, a movie theater, an art gallery, and a sports arena. The population was over 75,000. But we were heading to a one-stoplight town with only one sheriff and an old horse farm that had no horses and needed lots of tender loving care."

"Our trip to Iowa was almost 1,500 miles. We had to make frequent stops because we are women and women tinkle more than guys. Then there was "Meatball," my dog. He is a mutt. I insisted on keeping him and taking him to Iowa. The open air and cornfields would be a great place to chase critters."

"We finally got to grandma's farm. It was a rundown old country home with a wrap-around porch that looked inviting to sit for a while and ponder life. The house was three stories, with an attic topping the third level. It had a spiral stairway that creaked when you tried to use it. Of course, my room was on the third level. It was spooky and yet fun because I could see all over the farm and watch the stars pass on parade across the night sky."

"We settled in and grandma made some sandwiches and lemonade. It was stuffy in the house, so we sat on the porch and rocked the afternoon away, talking girl stuff and catching up on my life and Mary's financial status. It was a stressful time for me and even worse for Suzie because she had to fabricate lies as we talked so grandma would think she was Mary."

Jessie, Dear Diary…" Grandma seems nice. She does not look like the person Suzie said she is. I am concerned that I might do the wrong thing supporting Suzie."

"Grandma was not buying Suzie's impression of Mary. She called me aside later that day and said, "What is with Mary? She does not seem like herself. I have-not seen her in several years but what I remember differs from who she is today."

"I played along with Suzie's swindle, and let grandma know Mary was under a lot of stress because of me and that was why she was not herself. I told her about my pregnancy and the trouble with the Miami police."

"I got a big hug and lots of comfort from grandma with a word from the Bible that said in part that all things would work together for good to those who love God and are called according to his purposes." (Romans 8:28)

Jessie, Dear Diary…" God working out everything for my good? That is surely not me." Grandma must be a little off, or she has been drinking."

It was like grandma read my thoughts. She said, that could be you. All you need to do is believe in God, accept Jesus as your personal Savior and trust in him.

Jessie, Dear Diary, "Now, that was a tall order. I do not even know who God is. How can I believe in him, much less trust in an unseen mystical entity?"

Grandma, "I am so glad you are here. The farm has been in our family for over 100 years and now I am on the verge of losing it. After the war, times were hard. Most of the nation was still recovering from the perils of war. Iowa was no different. Jobs were hard to find and new business start-ups were far and few between.

It was as if we were all moving in slow motion towards somewhere we did not know. The future was unsure and the prospects for tomorrow were in serious question. But we survived and prospered as we prayed to God and put our trust in Jesus to get us through. If he helped us then, he will not forget us now."

"When I was your age, Jessie, 90% of Americans professed to be Christian. There was no mention of "Gay Rights", "Transvestites", "Women's Liberation", and other alternate lifestyles. We believed God prepared the rain for the earth so the crops could grow. Our belief was that men marrying men and girls living with a man or engaging in premarital sex was wrong. Before: Instead of pleasing ourselves, we were God-fearing and sought to please him. We did not kill our unborn children in the name of good health. We saw life as a relationship with God, not the fad or the fashion of the day."

"Now, the government is about to take all of this away because of my default on taxes over the last five years."

Jessie, Dear Diary… "I laughed to myself, saying, this farm is not worth much in its current condition. Maybe she should sell it."

"Suzie left for a few days to visit some friends in a neighboring town. That left me and grandma to talk and we did that for sure. We sat on the porch for hours discussing mostly religious things. I felt comfortable with my grandma and asked questions about life, death, morality, truth and just about everything else."

Grandma, says Jessie, "why do I exist? Why am I here living on earth now?"

"Good question, said grandma. I questioned that for years until I became a Christian and read the Bible. I read in Genesis that God created man, male, and female and gave them authority to rule over his earth. I came to realize that I was not a mistake, or a product of evolution. God created me in his image and likeness as a special creation. That tells me God does not make junk."

Jessie, "Does that mean God looks like us?

Grandma, "No honey, it means that he put into us his character so we would look like him and could enjoy his life and experience all that he is."

Jessie, "Character?"

Grandma says, "Yes, we inherited his nature." That would be love, joy, peace, kindness, and many other godly attributes. God placed these attributes into Adam and Eve when he made them. That is why abortion, suicide, and murder are wrong. We should not destroy what God has made.

Jessie, "ok then, why don't I have any of these Godly things? Why was I left out? What is the matter with me? Does God not like me?"

Grandma, "Your rebellion and attitudes did not start with you. Adam and Eve were the first human beings to rebel against God. They had all the blessings of God and even possessed his character. God created them without sin. But when they rebelled so they could be their own gods, he withdrew his Spirit and they fell into an evil nature that was against God. When they fell from God's presence, so did their descendants. That includes us. We were born into sin and have a nature, not after God, but evil."

"That is why Jesus died on the cross at Calvary. He

died in our place as the penalty for our rebellion against God. Now we can live for him and walk in his character like Adam did in the beginning. God created us in his image and likeness. When we accept Jesus as our savior, he fills us with his Spirit and we can know him and worship him. He becomes the reason for our living here on earth and our doorway into eternity when we die."

Jessie, "That is a lot to handle right now. Can I think about it for a day or so?

Grandma, "Of course, my dear."

Suzie, I mean Mary… "Hi grandma., I am back from Cedar Rapids. Is everything alright?

Grandma, "Yes honey, all is well. We have been talking about God and how he loves us so much that he sent Jesus so we could see what God is like and so we could repent and come to him."

Suzie, "Jesus was not God. He was just a man like all the rest."

Grandma, "That is not what the Bible says. The Bible says he was and still is God in the flesh. He said, "If you have seen me, you have also seen the Father, for he and I are one." He also said that the Father sent his only son, referring to himself, that whosoever believes in him will have eternal life." We need to believe in him and make him our Savior."

Jessie, "Can we change the subject now? I want to pick through all the antiques in the basement."

Jessie, Dear Diary…" All this religious talk. I am stressed out over it. I wish grandma would lighten up."

"Hey grandma", says Jessie, there is a police car in

our drive and two men with white coats. I guess they are here for me. I will let them in."

Grandma, "can I help you, officer?"

Jessie, "I guess you are here for me. I will go quietly."

Suzie, "I am Mary, Jessie's mother. What do you want with her?"

Police Officer, "It is you we have come for." (The police officer cuffed Mary and the two men in white coats took her away.)

Police Officer, "Mary escaped from an insane asylum in Miami three days ago. She told another patient that she was going to run and would head here. She is serving 1-5 years of intense therapy for attempting suicide. Her complete loss of reality calls for urgent help. We will take her back and see that she gets all the help she needs."

Grandma, "Jessie? What is going on? Mary did not seem sick.

Jessie says, "Grandma, there is something I need to tell you." That lady was not my mother. Well, she said she was, but her name was Suzie, Mary's twin sister.

The real Mary, (several hours later) "Hi grandma, glad to see you and Jessie. For a while, I thought I had lost you forever. Let's get inside and if anyone comes looking for me, I am not here, ok?"

Grandma, "The police were here a few hours ago and took Mary, or whoever her name was, away, back to the insane asylum. What is this about a twin?

Jessie, "That lady told me she was Suzie, Mary's

twin sister and that I was really her child and not yours. She said that you and grandma forced her to give the baby, me, to Mary and then you ran her off. She said you raised me but I was really her child and that was why she showed up, to take me back and punish grandma.

Mary, "That's nuts. Grandma never had twins. I was the only child."

Grandma, "That is right. There was no twin."

Jessie, "But she showed me a birth certificate and a photo when you both were about five. Now I do not know who or what to believe."

Grandma, "Come with me, child. Now, open this picture book. See all the pictures? There are no twins, just your mother, you, me, and your grandpa. Turn the page. See that birth certificate? It has just one name on it: Mary.

Mary, "I lost Tom in the war and shortly after gave birth to you. I guess I blamed you for destroying my life. Without Tom, we had no family, and you were just a sad reminder that my life was in shambles. That is why I attempted suicide. I could not live with the guilt anymore."

Grandma, "wait a minute you two! God does not make mistakes. Jessie was a special blessing to you, Mary. He wanted you to have some of Tom in Jessie so you would not forget him. She is so much like her dad. Don't you see him in her? I do."

Mary, "I know that living here with grandma will give us a chance to start over and be the family that Tom wanted."

Jessie, "What about Suzie, the fake twin?"

Mary, "She is where she belongs. She can live out being me, but it will have to be in the asylum.

Jessie, "Well, I swiped her wallet with all your credit cards, driver's license, and other identification. I guess that gives you back your identity. The asylum has their Mary, and now we have ours. They will not be looking anymore.

Suzie (In the Asylum), "Ok, I will tell you why I picked Mary to swindle. I was in the grocery store and as I came to the front of the store to check out, I saw Mary in front of me. She looked at me and I looked at her and we both agreed that there was a striking resemblance. We could have passed for twins. That started a conversation that led to a nearby restaurant where we talked for hours. Good thing we bought nothing that was perishable."

Suzie continues, "At the restaurant, Mary told me about her daughter, Jessie, and all the trouble she was having with her and her grandma, the farm, and how they found oil on a neighbor's farm. She also talked about her wanting to kill herself. It was the perfect opportunity to assume her identity and take over. That is what I did. I jumped in head first and it would have worked if grandma had not become suspicious."

Asylum doctors responding, "What a story. You can really spin a yarn, lady. You expect us to believe all that? We met your grandma, and she said she never had twins. She also said you needed a lot of help and thanked us for caring. You will just have to stay here with us until you can get it straight and your grandma verifies your story. Meanwhile, we will continue the shock treatments, drugs, and counseling.

Suzie, "No, please, I am telling you the truth."

Doctors, "Take her back to her room. We will give her some time to rest and think about what really happened."

Jessie, Dear Diary…" I feel bad about Suzie. I shouldn't, but I do."

CHAPTER FOUR
THE APPLE TREE MYSTERY

GRANDMA, "FOR THE LAST FOUR years, I have been growing apple trees. Iowa is one of the best places to grow apples. The state supplies 10% of the nation's apples. It takes about four years before you get a big crop. This year should be our chance for a bumper crop and get us out of debt. We can harvest from late August through late fall.

Mary, "What type of apples are you growing?

Grandma, "I planted seven different types that grow better in Iowa than other states. It will take some work to pick all the apples because I planted 20 trees of each kind. There are 140 apple trees in the orchard. That is really a small orchard. Iowa has 1148 acres of apple trees. I have my hands full chasing rabbits, squirrels, and other critters away from the trees. They like to eat the leaves of the trees as they grow in the spring. Jessie? I am going to give you and your dog the responsibility to care for the apple orchard."

Jessie, "But grandma, I know nothing about apples."

Mary, responding to Jessie, "You will learn. It will be a glorious adventure. You can be the family's apple consultant and expert." Your dog, "Meatball," can keep the critters away."

Grandma, "You will learn. I have books that will help you and we can go to the local university, where they experiment with apple trees for more help if we need to. One of my favorite apples is the crabapple. I have 20 of this kind of tree in the orchard."

Mary, "But grandma, aren't they bitter tasting?"

Grandma, "Not these. They have an abundance of sugar in them and are very sweet. They are perfect for pies and just eating as a mid-day snack. This apple is smaller than the rest, but still good."

Mary, "Well, summer came and slowly drifted into fall. Cold weather arrived early and our orchard was full of apples. Jessie found a purpose for living and moved away from wanting to kill herself. I also started to heal from the many years of sorrow over the loss of Tom. Frost was on the ground, and the overnight forecast was for snow flurries. But that was the perfect condition for bringing the apples to maturity. We had to hire day laborers to help with the picking."

"Grandma already had a buyer for as many bushels as she could harvest. However, there is something strange going on in the orchard. There is one tree that is taller than the others and it has twice as much fruit on it as the other trees. There is an abundance of apples on that one tree. I want to know why. Is this an act of God or just an unusual weird thing?"

"As I thought about the mystery of the apple tree, grandma started attending a little country church. We went with her and they enrolled me in the youth group." I met some kids my age and made a few friends. Mister Jenson, the youth leader, was nice, so it was not so bad. Later, Mr. Jenson opened the youth meeting to questions. I immediately raised my hand and asked my apple tree mystery question. Why would God make one tree grow taller than all the rest and fill it with way more apples than all the rest in the orchard?"

Mr. Jenson, "I can answer that, but first, let's open it up to all the kids. Does anyone want to guess at the reason? Can we really know the reasoning behind what God does?"

Jessie, "The group came up with several reasons:

- Because God likes apples.

- Because there is a need for more apples.

- Because God wanted us to question his handiwork.

Mr. Jenson, "Let us go to the Bible to see if we might find a word from God. He can answer our question, I think. See if this makes any sense:

Here is what the apostle Paul says to the 1st century Christian community at Rome. "For the invisible things of him from the creation of the world are clearly seen, being understood by the things that are made, even his eternal power and Godhead; so that they are without excuse." Romans 1:20. This Bible verse tells us that God, who is invisible, can be seen by those things that he made, meaning creation. Apple trees are part of his creation. He can use one or all of them to reveal himself."

Jessie, "So what is the apple tree saying to us about God?"

Mr. Jenson, "I think the tree is saying several things. Consider these:

- God is all powerful. After all, he can make trees that produce apples. I cannot, can any of you?

- You cannot put God in a box of narrow expectations. We like everything to be equal, like every tree the same, but God breaks out of that mold and does it differently.

- God is our provider, giving us apples to eat, make pies and use to bless others.

Now, let us look at what Jesus says in John 10:10 "The thief comes not, but for to steal, and to kill, and to destroy: I am come that they might have life, and that they might have *it* more abundantly." He compares himself with the evil one, and says the thief or the devil shows up in our lives to steal and to kill, but he is here, in our lives, so we can experience life and have it in abundance."

"Here is what this verse says to me… God is a giver and when he gives, it is more than enough, but the devil is not a giver. He is a taker and he will steal our joy, take away our future, and kill our dreams."

Jessie, "So the mystery of the larger apple tree is God loving us so much that he blesses us with an abundance of apples to show his love and concern for our wellbeing? Am I correct?"

Mr. Jenson, "yes, when we see such an abundance of blessing, we can see the hand of God. It is a sign given to us by nature that reveals the love of God. But guess what? All the other trees are also full of fruit as part of the total blessing to show us the nature of God.

The extra on that one tree is just a stamp of approval to get our attention."

"One other thing, God is a God of variety. He does not create one of each species. That is why there are many types of flowers, trees, apples, animals and even people.

With people, God is no respecter of persons. That means he does not favor one race over another. There is no super race. There is no one that God loves more than another. We are all loved equally by God. He blesses some more than others, but it is not based upon our efforts. His blessings are always in accordance with his divine purposes and destiny. Racial hatred is not of God. God's favor is unmerited, meaning we can do nothing to get it. God freely gives it to all who believe in Jesus as their Savior.

CHAPTER FIVE:
THE DOMINO EFFECT

G RANDMA, "As the snow flies in the cold Iowa wind, Jessie, Mary, and myself hurry to the orchard to gather the last remnants of fallen apples. I felt that freshly fallen fruit was still good for the family's use. While searching for fallen apples, Jessie saw an injured colt standing under one of the apple trees. He was pushing the snow around looking for apples. Jessie slowly offered an apple to the colt, and he came up to her and took the fruit. He was cold and shivering."

"Jessie had a rope in the wagon she used to transport the apples from the orchard to the barn. She gently placed it over the horse's head and quickly gave it another apple. Then Mary pulled the wagon while Jessie walked the colt into the barn and stalled it, using the apples to keep it moving."

"The colt had no brand on it except for a distinguishing domino marking on its forehead. Jessie grabbed a blanket and covered the colt and then looked for the medical kit so she could care for the horse's leg injury. As far as they could tell, a wolf, or possibly a bear, attacked the colt."

Jessie stayed up all night with the colt, caring for its wounds and brushing its coat. The two formed a bond that night that made Jessie feel loved and accepted.

Over the next several weeks, Jessie lived in the barn. She would have set a place at the dinner table for the colt if we would allow it. She called the colt "Domino," because of the marking on its forehead."

Jessie, Dear Diary…" I hope grandma will allow me to keep this horse. I have always wanted a horse, but mom always said it would not be in this lifetime."

Grandma, "Domino became the subject of every discussion. He was everything to Jessie. He followed her around the farm like a little puppy dog. We looked for an owner but could not find one. No one lost a colt. So, we allowed Jessie to be the trainer of the colt and to care for all its needs."

"Domino had an unusual effect on Jessie. He showed her unconditional acceptance and love that no human had ever given her. We watched as Domino chipped away at Jessie's low self-esteem and poor self-confidence. He did nothing but be himself, but that seemed to be just what Jessie needed."

"Domino trusted Jessie to care for him, and that trust taught her to trust others and rely on the love of her family. Soon, she trusted in the truth of God's Word. That led her to face reality and deal with her emotional issues, which were many."

"The biggest thing I saw was how Domino helped Jessie reduce the anxiety that kept her trapped in a world of fear and depression. She began to relax and live life as an ordinary teen. Domino was better than any counselor. The therapy Jessie received was far better than any doctor, and it cost no more than a few apples, a bag of oats, and some hay twice a week."

Jessie, "I loved Domino, and he loved me. I would ride my bike down the country roads and he would follow me. We would stop at the stream for a drink and enjoy the fresh air together. I could tell him everything and he never criticized me or made me feel bad. He would just nudge my hand as if to say, "It's alright" and then sniff around for a carrot or an apple.""

"I saw the hand of God in Domino. He watched over me and was gentle around me. He listened to me and paid attention to my desires. I felt God's love and knew that he was on my side. Domino showed me how to love and how to trust. My grandma's unseen God became visible, and it was amazing."

"I saw God everywhere; In creation, in family life, in friends, in various situations, and especially in Domino. Then I read in the Bible where Jesus said he would never leave us or forsake us. That he would be with us even until the end of the world."

"Domino helped me let go of the past with all the drama and anxiety. He showed me how to relax and have fun. My grandma praises God for bringing Domino to her farm and she thanks him every day for "The Domino Effect" that saved my life.

"There was one other situation. I was walking home from school one day when I saw Domino running along the fence on our side of the dirt road that led to our farm. I met him and jumped over the fence to be with him. We walked for a while until we came up on two boys that tried to get to my horse to harass it. I pushed them away, and they persisted. I grabbed a big stick and hit one boy in the back. The other punched me in the face and I fell. Then the boys tried to molest me, but Domino would not let that happen. He kicked them until they ran off.

Those two boys told the sheriff that Domino attacked them and he needed to be put down. The issue went to court, and Domino's future was now on trial. When I presented my case to the judge, showing him my bruise and explaining that they hit me in the face and tried to molest me, he dismissed the case. The two boys faced charges of statutory rape. From then on, the kids at school called me "Super Teen" because I stood up to the two bullies. I could see God protecting me, using a horse to keep me from danger. I learned that day that God was greater than two bullies."

"Domino somehow saw the hurt in my soul and loved me, anyway. He treated me like a somebody, even though I was just an angry teen. Grandma said that is how God is. He sees our faults, knows our sin, feels our pain, and still loves us anyway."

CHAPTER SIX
GRAMMA AND THE
100-YEAR FARM

MARY, "THE OLDEST SON HAS managed the farm for over 100 years. However, the farm was and is the property of all born into the family. Because there are no family survivors other than grandpa Joe, he became the sole heir and last male to own the land. It has changed hands five times so far. Now, the farm will pass on into the hands of the oldest relative, be it male or female. Since grandma had no sons, the farm will pass down to me, the only daughter. Should Jessie have a son, he will be the rightful heir in the future, after it passes on to Jessie after my death."

"Uncle Joe, who passed away this year, inherited the farm from his father and so on back through time to before Iowa declared statehood. Iowa became a state in December 1846. Back then, our family owned and farmed 140 acres, but over the years, we had to sell off most of that to survive. We still own 40 acres of the best part of the land."

"If we cannot pay the bills, we might have to turn the 40 acres into eight, five-acre hobby farms and sell them to city folk in Cedar Rapids. The apple orchard has really helped to meet our needs so far, but that could change with just one bad year."

Jessie, "Wait a minute. When I took Suzie's purse

to save your identity, I found this letter. It is from the surveyor's office in Cedar Rapids. It says, the possibility of finding oil on our land is over 85%."

Grandma, "Iowa is not a crude oil-producing state and does not have any oil reserves. Of over 100 exploratory wells drilled in the state, only a handful ever produced oil. The chances are slim that a well on our land would be a producer."

Mary, "We could still investigate the possibility. You never know and we do not have to put up any money because the oil company covers the expenses, and we receive a percentage of what is sold."

Grandma, "Ok, we will investigate that."

Jessie, "Why are we worrying? Didn't you say, grandma, that God works everything out for good to those that love him and are called according to his purposes? If that is true, all we must do is let him do his thing. We will not have a terrible year with the orchard and if we do, God will provide another source of funding so we do not lose the farm. Isn't that right, Grandma?"

Grandma, "Yes, Jessie, that is right. I am glad you are seeing the promises of God. We all need to see them and believe them, even when things are not so great."

Jessie, "What were my grandpas like? I never knew grandpa Joe or any of those in the 1800s."

Grandma, "Well let's see, your grandpa Joe was a kind man. He worked hard to keep up the 40 acres we have now. Planting and harvesting were an all-day thing. There was no eight-hour shift and home for dinner and T.V. It was from sun up to sun down. This was seven days a week. We took a break to attend church and then he went back to the fields. There was no extra money to hire workers."

"Back in the 1800s, settlers fought Indians and the harsh winters. However, the Indians also fought among themselves. There were many tribes that occupied the land. Times were tough and people were tougher. They had to be to survive."

"Your grandpa, Joe, was one of eleven boys. There were three girls too. The Indians took three of his brothers and one girl died of consumption. People needed large families to care for and protect the land. We were the only couple that could not have a large family. I was not supposed to have children. The doctors told us it just cannot happen because of a medical issue that happened in my childhood. Guess what? They were wrong because I gave birth to you, Mary. You were an answer to my prayers. You were my miracle baby. You were and still are my blessing from God."

"There are over 50 people laid to rest in our family graveyard. All of them lived, worked, and died on this farm. They were pioneers searching for a new life that was full of God's grace. All of them trusted in Jesus and believed that he was God's only begotten Son, sent to save their souls."

"They trusted God for rain to grow the crops; protection against drought and harsh winters and, yes, even Indians. We have a great heritage and a lasting testimony to the love of God that has blessed our family for over 100 years." God has been there for us every day from the time we trusted him and he will not abandon us now, in our time of need."

"According to our family history, we almost lost the land in 1879 when lightning struck the barn and quickly spread to the outbuildings. The historical account mentioned that smoke was visible for miles and the surrounding forest also caught fire. God's help came quickly with a rainstorm that came out of nowhere. It quenched the forest fires and cooled the heat in the barn. The family lost livestock, stored crops, and valuable farming equipment. But they lived and, with the help of their neighbors, made it through until things got better."

Jessie, "Here comes, "Meatball" Hi little doggy. He just loves the farm. He chases the chickens, rolls in the dirt with the pigs, and loves to go after rabbits and squirrels. Did all our ancestors have dogs?"

Grandma, "They sure did. Grandpa Ben, who lived in the 1890s, raised dogs. He introduced sheep to the community instead of cows. The neighbors thought it was foolish, but he did it anyway. To herd them, he raised border collies and even sold a few to the town folk for cattle management. The sheep did well and prospered, even in the cold weather. Wool is a major thing these days. However, when grandpa Ben died, his son, Sam, sold off most of the livestock and went back to farming. Sam sold the dogs to other sheep herders."

"Various battles of the Civil War claimed the lives of some of our relatives. Some of our relatives received decorations for their courage. Iowa was pro Abraham Lincoln, supporting the efforts of the Union. However, there was one son that supported the South. They caught him passing documents to the rebels and hanged him as a traitor."

"Our family has survived floods, fires, predators, drought, tornados, wars, and even corrupt governments. We have put our lives into this land and it will stay ours as long as we fight for it. God will be there for us. We just need to keep on keeping on and trusting the Lord to make it all happen."

Jessie, "Grandma? Where did our ancestors come from?

Grandma, "Our family migrated to the United States in the early 1800s. They came from Europe, specifically Germany. Revolutionary wars and rebellion against the existing rule led them to flee. They brought with them the skills for making beer. It was their livelihood once they settled down. They came thru the "New York Port of Call" and immediately headed west. It was common knowledge that the mid-west had lots of open land with rich soil where they could grow the crops for brewing beer. By the time Iowa became a state, our family had already settled on the 140-acre plot east of what is now Cedar Rapids."

"The Germans were the largest immigrant population in Iowa in the mid-1850s. They were in competition for land with native American Indians, The French, Swedish and other nationalities, all who were fleeing their own countries for various reasons. Some were looking to get rich. Others running away from war, food shortages, religious persecution, and tyrannical dictators."

Jessie, "So we have a lot to live for, right?"

Grandma, "Right!"

Jessie, "Hear that mom? No more thoughts of suicide. If I must live and be a good little girl, so do you. The three of us must join forces and face the future. It's like what the youth leader said in church. He said, "If we keep our eyes on the past, we will never see what is in front of us and probably miss God's blessings.""

Grandma, "I agree with that. We then will face the future together and make our farm a great place to grow up and enjoy the blessing of God. Look out, world. Here come the three ladies from Springville."

Jessie, Dear Diary…" I feel good about the future. I hope it all works out."

CHAPTER SEVEN
BOYFRIENDS, HORSES, AND VALUES

JESSIE, "I FAILED THE 7TH grade because I was out too much and missed the teaching. However, they allowed me to attend summer school, so I made up for all the missed classes and successfully moved on to the eighth grade. I was now 14 years old. I was developing into a woman and getting lots of looks from boys at school. Even the boys in my youth group were hovering over me with funny looks and smiles. I guess they thought I was cute.

I began getting asked out on dates. My calendar was full for Friday and Saturday nights for months. When I told my mom about all the attention, she and grandma sat me down for a girl talk about the birds and the bees. I already gave birth to my baby, an 8-pound beautiful boy. I named him Joe, after my grandpa because grandma said he was kind and that was what I wanted for my child."

Grandma, "Now Jessie, we realize you were sexually active and did things that were immoral. Running with a gang and being sexually involved has grown you up a lot faster than other kids your age. Never-the-less, you can still go back to being a teenager by starting over. The folks in Iowa know nothing about your past but what you tell them. Say nothing and they will accept you as an ordinary teen, like them."

"Now, I want to discuss values. A suitable set of values will restore your dignity and strengthen your self-worth. With values, there are only two paths to travel. You can travel down the immoral path or take the high road of morality. In the past, you chose the wrong path and got pregnant and ended up with the police after you. That will not happen if you take the high road and decide to be a moral person."

"These teenage boys want you to be immoral, so they can use and abuse you. God wants you to be moral so he can bless you with the right guy that will love you and not put you down. But, let's set God's will aside for now and look at some things that you have or will face in the upcoming years. We will just use common sense to evaluate their worth and benefit."

"The 1st is pre-marital sex…You get stuck with the baby and the boy goes off to impregnate another unaware girl. Plus, there is always the chance of getting a venereal disease. Having a kid while you are a kid is hard. You found that out firsthand. Most girls with a kid lose their friends because they grow up faster and develop different interests."

"2ND is drugs…Forget what happened in the past. Look at the results of a drug addict. Giving up on life is what they do. They live for the next fix. They will do anything to get high so they can function. This is not a lifestyle for your future. It will destroy you and your dreams."

"3RD is language. Before, when you were in the

gang, your language was full of bad words that were offensive to most people. Being a lady requires a clean vocabulary that promotes you as a person of integrity. Doing otherwise causes you to be low class and is a sign that you are easy or willing to be immoral."

"4TH is Gossip…If you are in a group that gossips, rest assured that they will gossip about you when you are not around them. Gossip has destroyed reputations, broken relationships and is a mean attack against those who suffer under it."

"5TH is lying… Lying is the opposite of telling the truth. God hates liars because they bear false witness and their accusations are motivated by evil."

"6Th is stealing…When you steal, you deprive someone else of having what you took, be it money, cars, property, or even boyfriends. Greed and selfishness motivate those who steal. It is illegal and can get you jail time."

"7Th is smoking cigarettes. They cause cancer of the lungs and leave a terrible smell on your clothes. Stay away from them and try not to date anyone that smokes."

"I am sure there are more, but I will let you decide what they are. The point is, none of these vices bring you lasting benefits. They are not of God and are never in his divine plan for you. It is always better to resist actions that cause evil to thrive and look for a moral or godly replacement that will bless you over the years."

Mary, "Now that we have discussed values, let us talk about boyfriends. I will not restrict you from dating because of your history with boys. However, there will be some guidelines, so we know you are safe and can help you if you get into trouble. I made a list. Here we go:"

- No sex or petting.

- Be in at the time we agree upon.

- No individual dating until you are 16.

- Group dates only like in the youth group or school activity.

- Come straight home after a movie or school event unless there is a responsible adult chaperone with you.

- No going steady for right now. I want you to date several boys so you can judge their character and evaluate them as a good or bad influence.

- Have fun but keep your dignity and show a little class.

Grandma," We are glad that Domino is with us. You have taken good care of him. However, as you get more involved with boys here in Iowa and school activities, you may push Domino aside. He must be your priority. He is a living thing and requires your time. Your baby will also take up more time. These two come before boys and dating. You are not a footloose and fancy-free kid anymore. You are a responsible teen mother with obligations and duties to fulfill. That being said, we will help as much as we can, but you must bear the load."

Jessie, "I realize what I did wrong and I know how to make it better. I have changed since being here.

Domino has loved me and accepted me from the minute he wandered on to the farm. I am happy for the first time. I guess God really does love me. He sent Domino to me and helped mom to feel better about herself and gave us you, grandma, to encourage us. I can feel the presence of the Lord here at the farm."

CHAPTER EIGHT:
GRAMMA'S BIBLE, BUTTERFLIES, AND GOD

JESSIE, "GRANDMA, I HAVE A question. What do I say when the kids at school laugh at me and say, "everybody does it…It's ok." Because I do not run with them like I did with the gang, they think I am a "Goody Two-Shoes." It is like I am swapping one gang for another, and the new gang is just as bad. The school crowd hides their true feeling and are two-faced. The old gang was honest about how they felt. What do I say?"

Grandma, "Well, let me ask you a question? Do you want to fit in with the new gang? Do you need their acceptance to be happy? That gang is on a road that leads to eternal destruction. They seek instant pleasures at any cost. Being a Christian is to walk on the narrow road with Jesus, which will lead straight into the kingdom of God."

"What I would tell them is, "I follow Jesus, and everybody is not doing the things that you are. Some of us want to please God and want to live a moral lifestyle." If you want to go further, you can add…everyone will one day stand before God and give an account for their actions. I want to stand before God with a clean heart and a clear conscience."

"There is another thing to watch for. When I was

young, the kids said, "Who says it is wrong?" My answer is God. He says it is wrong in the Bible or through just laws that govern the affairs of men. That is how I know I should not take part. Plus, there is an unction in my spirit from God telling me to avoid this subject or activity."

"I listen to my conscience that reveals the will of God. Then I do what is right. This is for my benefit and protection. Evil forces will always challenge what is right. They will force you to justify your actions. If you do not know what God wants and what he says is right, you will fall under their accusations. That is why we study the Bible and learn all the truth we can, so we can use it against any accusation that comes our way."

Jessie, "I am not sure I understand."

Grandma, "Here is an example straight from the Bible in the words of Jesus. He said, "It is written." Jesus used this phrase to withstand attacks from the devil when he was being tempted in the wilderness. On one occasion, he said, "It is written, man does not live by bread alone, but every word that precedes out of the mouth of God."

"The attack was to turn a stone into bread and eat it to satisfy his hunger. The deception was to use his power as the Son of God outside the will of his Father. You can use scripture to resist evil by saying what Jesus said, "It is written." If you do the same by quoting scripture to the voice in your head or people that say things that are against the will of God for you, then you will be okay.

"The Bible is God's word to us. The Holy Spirit

inspired it and it is good for correcting us when we are wrong, helping us to know what is right and living life in his will. Some folks claim they cannot rely upon the Bible because it is out of date. That is just not true.

The Bible is a living word that guides the believer through good and bad times. It is a fascinating book to read. Among its contents are mysteries, drama, battles, discussions on human relationships, marriage, life and death issues, forgiveness, rewards, faith, hope, love, and more. Its central theme is the redemption of mankind by a loving God who created them. If you look hard as you read, you may even get a glimpse of God Himself and learn who he is.

"What am I trying to say? Only this:"

- We can trust the Bible as our only true source of Godly knowledge and wisdom.

- We can draw from the Bible, faith, hope, and spiritual growth.

- We can communicate with God, gaining direction and leadership.

- We can see Jesus through the gospels, miracles, prophecy, and poetic psalms.

Do not allow anyone to discredit the Bible. What they say against it is a lie. They are trying to destroy your bond with God and drive you away from the love of Jesus."

Grandma continues, "Well, I have shared my beliefs, which are grounded in the promises of God and found in the Bible. I want to pass those promises to you so that you will have a strong foundation to stand on when you face life's challenges."

"Now, both of you need to be "Born Again." If you do not get born again, you will not see the kingdom of God, much less enter it after you die. It is time for both you, Jessie, and your mother to decide to accept Jesus as your Savior or reject him and go your own way. Life is too short to dilly dally in this world."

Jessie, "How can I be born again? I am already born. That sounds silly, grandma."

Grandma, "That's ok Jessie. Many folks do not know what it means to be "Born Again" Even Christians are at a loss to describe the born-again experience, much less admit that they have experienced it. Being "born again" is about embracing God's grace, receiving forgiveness, and entering a new life in Christ."

"There is a metaphor seen in nature that depicts this experience. It is the Butterfly. As you may know, the butterfly undergoes a miraculous transformation from a caterpillar into an entirely new creature. So it is with the human soul. It undergoes a transformation from evil to righteous; from darkness to light; from death to life.

I wrote this poem a while back and I want to read it to you."

BE A BUTTERFLY

Be a Butterfly
And fly away with me.
We'll fly on God's Promises
Right into eternity.

Be a Butterfly
To crawl no more.
But to soar in the Spirit
Above earth's mighty roar.

Be a Butterfly
To fly to heights unknown.
Soaring on the wings of faith
Never more to be alone.

Be a Butterfly
And fly away with me.
For God has made us new
At last! At last! We are free.

"Being born again is necessary for us to become the new creature that God has planned for us. The main reason for us to be born again is because it is our divine destiny. It is the will of God. It is the only way we will see heaven, Jesus, and all the saints. This is the pathway to God, the Father. Being "Born Again" has personal benefits for believers. I can think of eight benefits off the top of my head."

- "The primary benefit is salvation. When a person is born again through faith in Jesus Christ, they receive forgiveness of their sins and receive the promise of eternal life. Our new birth marks the beginning of a transformed relationship with God."

- "The Holy Spirit indwells all believers, empowering them to live a life that reflects God's character. New desires and godly attitudes replace our old habits."

- "Through the new birth, we receive a new identity. We become children of God, adopted into his family. Our status changes from being spiritually dead to being alive in Christ."

- "We, as Born-again believers, experience freedom from the bondage of sin. The power of sin is broken, and we can now overcome temptations through the power of God and the guidance of the Holy Spirit."

- "God has a unique purpose for each one of us. Being born again opens the door to discovering and fulfilling that purpose. We are called to serve

God and others, using our God-given gifts and talents for his glory."

- "Our new birth assures us of God's unwavering love. We know nothing can separate us from his love." (Romans 8:38-39).

- "We become part of the global family of believers. We can find fellowship, encouragement, and support from other followers of Jesus."

- "We, as "Born Again" believers, experience a sense of purpose and fulfillment that transcends earthly circumstances. The hope of eternal life and the joy of knowing Christ bring deep satisfaction."

"Remember that being born again is not a mere ritual; it is a profound transformation of the heart and soul. Jesus emphasized this truth when he said, "Truly, truly, I say to you, unless one is born again, he cannot see the kingdom of God" (John 3:3, ESV). It is an invitation to experience God's grace and enter a new life in Christ."

"It hurts me to read about people who claim to be Christian but do not want to be born again. They deceive themselves and follow the wrong path in life. I guess they believe that their church will save them or their good works or the fact that they are worthy in some other way to qualify for eternal life."

Mary, "Are you sure that Jesus is the only way?"

Grandma, "Yes, Mary, I am sure that Jesus is the only way." **"Just One Way"** It is hard for most folks that are not "Born Again" to understand why there is just one way to God, yet it is true. There is only one way, and that is through Jesus Christ."

The Bible is our source to prove that the one-way teaching is valid. Acts 4:12 says, "Neither is there salvation in any other: for there is none other name under heaven given among men, whereby we must be saved."

"Here is why it is so important. Adam sinned against God and died spiritually. "And the LORD God commanded the man, saying, of every tree of the garden thou may freely eat: But of the tree of the knowledge of good and evil, thou shalt not eat of it: for in the day that thou eat thereof thou shalt surely die." Genesis 2:16-17

"This creation account shows him being made of clay and God breathing into him the breath of life. He thus became a living soul. "And the LORD God formed man of the dust of the ground and breathed into his nostrils the breath of life; and man became a living soul." Genesis 2:7. When he sinned, he lost the breath of life, and he became a dead soul. He was truly the first of a race of the walking dead".

"Life is always in a relationship with God. It is his breath or Spirit that makes us alive. So, death passed upon all men for all sinned. (Romans 5:12) Their nature was now sinful. We see this in all of us and in our society."

"The 2nd birth experience is by the Spirit. The Spirit gives the "Breath of Life" to each repentant heart and awakens their soul to God. They become his children by birth."

"All the world religions cannot save us. Joining a church or specific faith cannot save us. It must be an acknowledgment of our sin, our cry before the throne of God for forgiveness, and our invitation for Jesus to come into our hearts and save us. His name is the only name that can get us through death into eternal life."

"If you doubt me on this, listen to these Bible verses."

…" there is one God, and one mediator between God and men, the man Christ Jesus; Who gave himself a ransom for all, to be testified in due time." (I Timothy 2:5-6)

…" believe on the Lord Jesus Christ and thou shalt be saved"… (Acts 16:31)

.. "that if thou shalt confess with thy mouth the Lord Jesus, and shalt believe in thine heart that God hath raised him from the dead, THOU SHALT BE SAVED. For with the heart man believes unto righteousness; and with the mouth confession is made unto salvation." (Romans 10:9-10)

"I know what you may think. "You mean to tell me that all the religions of the world are wrong and only Christianity is the one true religion?" Remember, Christianity is not a religion. It is a relationship born out of love between man and the one true and living God. There is no one true religion. Religion will not get us to God. It is the blood of Christ that unlocks the door and our confession of faith in Jesus that makes it all happen. "(John 14:6)

Jessie, Dear Diary…" We are really into it now. It is

too much to absorb all at once. I wish she would slow down."

Mary, "Grandma? Please slow down. It is getting heavy…too much to handle. You are losing us."

Grandma, "Ok Mary, but I just want to finish my thought. Just a few more things."

"Jesus is the only way to God because God planned it that way. He set the penalty for sin, which was death. The soul that sins, it shall die. (Ezekiel 18:20) In fact, Jesus was the slain Lamb of God before the foundation of the world." (Ephesians 1:3-7)

"Jesus Himself said, as recorded in John 14:6, "I am the way, the truth, and the life: No man comes to the Father but by Me". Christianity states that the God of the Bible is the only true God and salvation is only possible by accepting Jesus Christ, his only begotten Son as Savior and Lord. II Corinthians 5:21 said, "For he (God) has made him to be sin for us, who knew no sin; that we might be made the righteousness of God in him."

"God validated his Son as the only way to him in lots of different ways, so we could be assured that Jesus was indeed the only way to him. Here are some to consider."

- He claimed to be the only way, as in John's record 14:6 says, but validation came through miracles that proved he was who he claimed to be.

- Eyewitnesses saw Jesus' miracles and validated them as authentic. Over 500 followers saw Jesus after his resurrection and watched him ascend into heaven.

- The prophets foretold of his coming, where he would be born, that he would be God in human flesh and lots more…all prophetic statements were realized in Jesus, even those like in Isaiah chapter 53 that were uttered hundreds of years before Jesus came.

- God Himself validated Jesus as his sole pathway to him. "While he was still speaking, behold, a bright cloud overshadowed them; and suddenly a voice came out of the cloud, saying, "This is My beloved Son, in whom I am well pleased. Hear ye him!" (Mathew 17:5)

- The apostles lost their homes, wealth, and even their lives preaching the gospel. Would they do that if it were a lie? I do not think so. They testified to the truth and were willing to die for it.

- Thousands of believers, over several centuries, have testified to how Jesus helped them and blessed them.

- I can personally testify that I have seen the hand of the Lord in my life and communicate with him daily. I know he is the only way.

"Now I realize that the probability that one man could fulfill all prophecies about a Messiah that God Himself said would come, (Gen.3:15), and perform fantastic miracles while here on earth, and be raised from the dead, and ascend into heaven while hundreds looked on in astonishment. But Jesus did just that… fulfilled everything that was foretold about the coming Messiah."

He had to be who he says he was and, therefore, is truly the only way to God. (By the way…Messiah is a Hebrew word for, "Anointed One." and Christ is a Greek word for, "Anointed One.") Jesus is the Messiah and he is the Christ."

It should be obvious by now that it is essential for anyone who wants eternal life to be, "Born Again." Romans 10:9-10 will tell us how."

"That if thou shalt confess with thy mouth the Lord Jesus, and shalt believe in thine heart that God has raised him from the dead, thou shalt be saved. For with the heart man believes unto righteousness; and with the mouth confession is made unto salvation." Romans 10:9-10.

"Confessing Jesus is to acknowledge his Lordship and openly proclaim your allegiance. There is no secret society. That's why the scripture says, "With Thy Mouth."

"Believing with the heart is different from believing with the mind. When we believe with our heart, it means to rely upon, adhere to, and trust in. We are to wholly embrace the truth that God raised up Jesus from the dead after being crucified for the sins of humanity."

"The power to save us and birth us into his kingdom as his child is in the fact that our heartfelt belief brings us the righteousness of Christ and our open mouth of continual confession of him as our savior saves us."

"Remember what Paul wrote to the Romans in

Chapter 5. He said, in effect, that Adam was the 1st man who fell into sin and took the entire race with him. Thus, death passed upon all of us."

"However, Jesus was the 2nd Adam or last man that was sent outside of the pollution of human sinful DNA via a virgin birth to be the spotless Lamb of God and to be slain as a sacrifice for sin to abolish it forever. This is why the "New Birth" is necessary, to free us from the sin of the 1st Adam and propel us by spiritual birth into the kingdom of God."

Jessie, "How do we know for sure that we are, "Born Again?"

Grandma, The Bible says, "The Spirit itself bears witness with our spirit that we are the children of God: And if children, then heirs; heirs of God, and joint-heirs with Christ; if so be that we suffer with him, that we may be also glorified together." Romans 8:15-17.

"We can say that we are his children, without a doubt or any question in our minds. We can because the Spirit of God is continually bearing witness with our spirit. He leads us; He communicates with us; He teaches us and shows us truth and error. That is how we know for sure.

Mary, "How does this "Born Again" experience change us?

Grandma, "Again, the Bible says, "And you were dead in your trespasses and sins, in which you formerly walked according to the course of this world, according to the prince of the power of the air, of the spirit that is now working in the sons of disobedience. Among them, we too all formerly lived in the lusts of our flesh, indulging the desires of the flesh and of the mind, and were by nature children of wrath, even as the rest."

"But God, being rich in mercy, because of his great love with which he loved us, even when we were dead in our transgressions, made us alive together with Christ (by grace you have been saved), and raised us up with him, and seated us with him in the heavenly *places* in Christ Jesus, so that in the ages to come he might show the surpassing riches of his grace in kindness toward us in Christ Jesus."

"For by grace, you have been saved through faith; and that not of yourselves, *it is* the gift of God; not because of works, so that no one may boast. For we are his workmanship, created in Christ Jesus for good works, which God prepared beforehand so that we would walk in them. Remember that you were at that time separate from Christ, excluded from the commonwealth of Israel, and strangers to the covenants of promise, having no hope and without God in the world."

"But now in Christ Jesus you who formerly were far off have been brought nearby the blood of Christ. For he himself is our peace, who made both *groups into* one and broke down the barrier of the dividing wall, by abolishing in his flesh the enmity, *which is* the Law of commandments *contained* in ordinances, so that in himself he might make the two into one new man, *thus* establishing peace, and might reconcile them both in one body to God through the cross, by it having put to death the enmity."

"So then, you are no longer strangers and aliens, but you are fellow citizens with the saints, and are of God's household, having been built on the foundation of the apostles and prophets, Christ Jesus Himself being the cornerstone, in whom the whole building, being fitted together, is growing into a holy temple in the Lord, in whom you also are being built together into a dwelling of God in the Spirit." Ephesians 2:1-22 ASV

"This scripture tells us where we were or are now and where God takes us when we are Born Again. It is truly a life-changing experience. There are ten more benefits that overtake the believer at his new birth. They are:

- We experience God's great mercy and love.

- We are made alive to God and given eternal life.

- We were raised up with Christ and seated with him in heavenly places.

- We receive his grace or unmerited favor.

- We are brought close to God by the Blood of Christ.

- Jesus becomes our peace.

- We gain access to God through his Spirit.

- We are no longer strangers but fellow citizens and joint heirs with Christ.

- We are becoming a spiritual dwelling for God.

- We are his workmanship, created in Christ Jesus unto good works that were established before we were saved so we could walk in them."

"We have looked at benefits of being "Born Again"

and why it is necessary to attain eternal life. We have seen how to be "Born Again" through repentance, a plea for forgiveness and an invitation to Jesus to enter our hearts and be Lord over our lives.

There is only one thing left to do: decide if you are "Born Again" or not. If not, go before the Lord and ask to be born into his kingdom. Then follow the teachings of Jesus."

Grandma continues, "I guess I got carried away with my Bible teaching, but it is so very important that you, Mary and you Jessie, understand and can become children of God."

CHAPTER NINE
SEVEN THINGS
MOMMA SAID

J ESSIE, "MOM? WHAT DO YOU think about all that grandma said? She sure knows how to preach."

Mary, "My mother, said a lot of things. However, there were seven important truths that stuck in my mind."

- Momma said we should live our own life and not let others tell us what to do. That hits home with me because I have been hiding from life and not being me. My sorrow at losing your dad in the war has consumed me. Grandma showed me a better way to live and gave both of us hope.

- Momma said we should always be responsible for our actions. If we mess up, we should own up to it and pay the price. If we face hard life situations, we should embrace them and work through them. She said running away is not a solution.

- Momma said we should know who we are and never forget it. If someone asked, "Who are you? We should be prepared to respond with a godly reply.

- Momma wanted us to develop a relationship with

God and walk in his Spirit towards our divine destiny. She wanted us to realize that his will is above ours and we should follow him. He does not follow us.

- Momma said to study the Bible and put to memory those promises that are written for our benefit. They are our weapons to fight the evil forces that come against us.

- Momma says we should be "Born Again" so we will be with her in heaven. She wanted us to become children of God so he can bless us and keep us free from this world's folly.

- Momma said we are to love God and each other and pray for his guidance so we can keep the farm and continue our family heritage.

Mary continues, "When I was your age, Jessie, I could not wait to get away from this farm. It was not my cup of tea. Marrying Tom gave me the chance to run and run I did. His paycheck came to me because I was his wife. I moved to Miami, Florida because I wanted to be as far away as I could from your grandma and her old fashion ideas. There was a base in Homestead, Florida, and I could be close to Tom. It was there that I found out I was pregnant with you. Shortly after, I learned Tom was missing in action and presumed dead."

"Fortunately, Tom took out a military insurance policy for $10,000, naming me as beneficiary. Once they officially reported him killed in action, they sent me a check. I lived on it for a while, but it was not enough to sustain my needs as a pregnant mother. I went to work in a nearby ammunitions factory. I made 50 caliber machinegun bullets for the army."

"They let me take you with me to work. I worked the night shift. After the war, the factory shifted its focus and starting making electronic parts for missiles. They kept me on as a supervisor in quality control. I made sure the parts met government specifications."

"Then when the economy made a turn for the worst, I lost my job, and we moved to the Miami slums. I could have run home to Iowa but was too embarrassed. The slums looked better than the farm."

"Boy, was I wrong. That is where you got involved with that gang, and selling drugs. I am so sorry. I was foolish and almost lost you. If your grandma had not called me, I would have killed myself and left you in the gang wars."

Jessie, "Mom? What was daddy like? I never knew him. I have dreams about him but never able to see him clearly. He is just a shadow that haunts me."

Mary, "Your dad was a great guy. You would have loved him. We were high school sweethearts. I was in the 11th grade and he was a senior. We dated all the time. He would walk me to class and then ran to his so he would not be late. We had lunch together every day. It was my first genuine love, and it still lives in my heart, even though he is gone."

"Once he graduated, he went into the military and applied to be an officer and a pilot. He excelled in advanced mathematics, which helped him with flight school. He became an officer and the pilot of a B-29 bomber, and they shipped him to an unknown destination. I never saw him again."

"We were very much in love and planned for a glorious future with kids, a home of our own, a good job and all the benefits that our free society offered. The news of his death shattered our dreams and broke my heart. I died that day and stayed dead inside all these years until now. Your grandma has given us hope and a chance for the future to live again."

CHAPTER TEN
THE REST OF THE STORY

J ESSIE, "As I write this diary, ten years have passed. I call them the silent years when I grew up and became an adult. I was thirteen when I was that troubled teen, running away from the Miami police, God, and myself. A lot has happened, most of it for the good, thanks to my grandma."

"Mary, my mom, and I got "Born Again" and started our spiritual journey with Jesus. We discovered a new reality that was filled with God's love and fellowship. We are part of the local church and accepted in the community."

"Meatball, my dog and Domino, my horse are still with me. They enjoy the country and playing with each other. I have two pigs, some chickens, and a few goats. We are looking into adding more livestock, but are not sure what kind."

"I am dating now. My boyfriend is none other than the local sheriff. His name is Louis Fields. I met him at the new mall at Cedar Rapids about four years ago. We are planning to get married next year after I serve jail time in a Miami correctional facility. It is a long story, but here is what happened."

"Louis found an old wanted poster in his office. The person of interest was me. My picture was on the poster with a caption that said, "Wanted In Connection

With Gang Violence." Louis showed me the poster and wanted to know what happened."

"I told him the full story and admitted my wrong doing. I told him I was going to discuss this with him before we got married, but I guess it could not wait. I am not that person anymore, but, as my grandma said, "We must own up to our mistakes and pay the price. I could just see the Sunday newspaper headlines" ..." **Sunday School Teacher Goes To Jail."**

"I went back to Miami and surrendered to authorities. Louis was with me and acted as my legal advisor. I went to court, and the judge asked me one question. He said, "Why did you give yourself up? We would never have found you. The statute of limitations, which would have been up next month, would have saved you and you could have gone "Scott-Free."

"I responded by telling the judge that going free after seven years was not the issue. I was wrong, and I needed to clear my conscience and make restitution so I could continue to be a responsible citizen."

"The judge was lenient with me? He said that considering the time passed and my desire to make restitution, he would sentence me to six months in jail. I would serve my time in a minimum-security location. Then I saw the hand of God move on my behalf. The judge looked straight at me and said, "However, I will withhold activation of my judgment until the next time you appear in a Miami criminal court. You can go free." I hugged Louis, and we praised God together as we left the courtroom."

"My picture never made the Iowa newspaper and

only Louis knew about my past. The Miami court system filed me away for good with no punishment. Louis and I return home to Iowa to plan our wedding and start a family."

"Grandma is still with us. She is in her 90s and is hoping to see me get married. Going back to Miami and dealing with my past made her proud of me. She said it was the Christian thing to do."

"Last week, Louis met a lady that is a caterer. He and another police officer were having lunch in a restaurant and discussed our wedding. Louis was asking the other police officer to be his best man. The lady heard them talking and came over to their table, introduced herself and said she was just getting into the catering business and gave Louis a great deal to cater our wedding. She is going to show up at the rehearsal dinner with special food and drink. "

"Now that I have taken care of that, I can focus on my dress, guests, and decorations. We are planning to have the wedding in the barn. We are not going to the expense of renting tuxedos for the men and dresses for the bridesmaids. I planned to wear a nice dress. That will cut down on cost."

"We had no idea that we were about to experience a family tragedy. The past collided with our present and almost destroyed our future. The new caterer was that crazy lady that tried to pass herself off as Mary, 14-years ago. Her name back then was Suzie. She was plotting all these years to punish me for leaving her in the Insane asylum."

"She came with Jack, her boyfriend, to the rehearsal

dinner with no food. All she and her boyfriend had was a shotgun and two pistols. They both opened fire. Mary died instantly. Grandma remained unhurt but experienced a heartache from the trauma. Louis fired back and killed Suzie. My 14-year-old son grabbed a harvesting hand cycle that we kept in the barn and attacked Jack. Two other guests sustained non-serious injuries. Jack also died that day."

"I could not believe what was happening. My mother was dead and my grandma suffered a heartache. My wedding was just a week away. Guests had already received invitations, and many returned their RSVP cards. Grandma said we should go ahead with the wedding. It was what Mary wanted, so we did."

Jessie, Dear Diary…" How could I be happy when so much pain had ripped apart my soul?"

"I had to turn to God and ask Jesus to work everything out for good, as he said he would in Romans 8:28."

"Now I must face two issues. The first was dealing with the loss of my mother, Mary. Why was all of this happening? I could not help but cry out to God and said, "Why me, Lord?""

"Then there was my teenage son. He killed someone using deadly force. He took the life of another human being. How does he feel about that? Will he suffer under the trauma of this situation?"

Jessie, Dear Diary... "My heart is breaking. I worry so much. I need the peace of God to get me through. Why is all of this happening?"

"Once things settled down, grandma passed away.

Her heart just could not take the stress. So, I had a wedding and two funerals to take care of. Louis was helpful, but what do men know about staging a wedding and organizing two funerals?"

"Well, we made it through the wedding. All the guests tried to look happy and smiled at me, and said "Are you alright?"

"I was sad by my grandma's passing. She was a godly woman and a blessing to me, more than I could ever know. I am only 24 years old and know little about life. How am I going to run the farm, care for Joe, my son, and go on with my life? What about my new husband?"

Jessie, Dear Diary… "My soul is troubled about so many things. I see many painful days ahead?"

"I sat down with Joe and discussed the fact that he used deadly force against Jack and what that means. He was cool with it all because he said," it was in self-defense." He was defending his family against evil."

"Louis and I had many late-night talks about death and losing love ones. I guess it will just take time before things settle down. They say, "Time heals all wounds." I am not so sure that is a true statement, but it will have to do for now."

"Still left in my painful days was the handling of grandma's farm. It was mine now, and I had to manage it. I had a mandate from grandma to keep it in the family. However, Louis was a police officer. He knew nothing about farming. It will all rest on my shoulders. What to do? I pondered this matter for many days."

"I went out to the barn and brushed Domino. That

always helps me to think clearly. He is so kind and listens to me. I would give him carrots and he would nudge me for more. We spent hours together while Louis was at work. It really helped me because I finally came up with a plan to save the farm and insure its on-going existence."

Jessie, Dear Diary… "I am fearful that I might make the wrong decisions. How do I know that what I am doing is right?"

"I followed what grandma told me years ago. She said to allow the peace of God to lead you. If I do not have peace about doing this, I should move in another direction. But I have peace and so I will proceed with my new plan."

"I have 40-acres of which 30 are farmable. I will sublet them to neighboring farmers to grow crops and take a share of the harvest. That will bring in money every season and put food on the table. I have an apple orchard. I can harvest it every year as I have been, but I can also make and sell apple pies in the local market using grandma's recipe. She won the county fair's 1st prize three years straight for baking the best apple pie. With Louis's law enforcement income, and God's help, we will be fine. "

Jessie, Dear Diary... "I feel better about taking charge of the farm and going on into the future."

Louis, "Hey honey, guess what"? There was a reward for the capture of that crazy lady. It seems she hurt a lot of folks. I have a check made out to you for $50,000. Is that the hand of God or what? He loves us and has blessed us once again."

"Louis and I went through grandma's papers and personal things to clear out all her stuff. Louis found a sealed letter addressed to me marked, "Open only upon my death." Apparently, grandma still had things to say. However, this time, she would speak from beyond the grave. I told Louis to open the letter and read it to me."

Louis, "My dear Jessie, if you are reading this letter, I am dead and that is ok. I wanted you to know the truth about twins and your mother's husband. What I am about to tell you may seem bizarre, but it is true. All of it really happened."

"I really had twins. Mary and the crazy Suzie were identical twins. I raised both from birth to when Suzie became pregnant with Tom's child. Mary stole Tom away from Suzie. She did jump in and pushed Suzie aside."

"Tom did not know what Mary was doing. He thought he was with Suzie. She had the first date with Tom. Mary finally told him, but that was after she slept with him and announced that she was pregnant. However, she was not with child. She just said that so Tom would stop thinking about Suzie and accept her."

"Well, Suzie found out what Mary did and while Mary was out shopping one afternoon, Suzie went into Tom, as Mary and slept with him. She got pregnant with Tom's child. Tom did not know what happened or about the fight going on between the twins over him. He went off to war and was killed in action, so we thought."

"Suzie made me angry, but there was nothing I could do about it until a letter from the war department arrived at the house. The letter informed us that Tom was alive and that the war department would release him from a military hospital in a few weeks. Meanwhile, Mary had already taken the newborn baby, you, Jessie, as her own. Susie did not want her. She just wanted Tom, so I stepped in to solve the dilemma."

"I called the twins together and said to Suzie, "You get out and never come back. Jessie will stay with Mary. Mary did not know Tom was alive, and I never told her. I thought it was better for Mary to be sorrowful than to know Tom had rejected her and that he wanted Suzie."

"I told Suzie that Tom will remain dead to this family from now on. I destroyed all the photos of the twins and altered the birth certificate. Susie was dead to me."

"Jessie, my darling, your actual mother, was Suzie. She went off with Tom and lived a life of crime. Mary always believed that Tom had died in the war. She did not know that he was with Suzie all those years. Also, I recognized Susie's boyfriend, the guy with the gun that Joe killed. His name was not Jack. He was Tom, your father. He died at the hands of his own grandson."

"Forgive me for lying and hiding the truth. I was just trying to protect everybody. I did a poor job of that. May God forgive me" …. Signed…Grandma.

Jessie, Dear Diary…" What is going on? My son kills my father, with a harvesting sickle which I thought died in WWII. My newlywed husband kills my birth mother, who I never knew existed until a few months ago. To conceal her evil actions, my grandma resorted to lying and deceiving everyone. In a ten-minute gun battle, I lost my mother, my dad, my aunt, and shortly thereafter, my grandma. Can it get any worse? Where do I go from here?"

Louis, "Jessie? Let's give thanks to God that you did not get killed. One of those bullets had your name on it. I saw Suzie aiming at you when I shot her. By the grace of God, you are still breathing. We can make it together. God will help us overcome this tragedy and move on to a blessed future."

Jessie, Dear Diary… "I must look to Jesus. I am afraid, but I know God will turn this tragedy into a blessing."

"So, life goes on for the living and Jessie and Louis walked by faith into an uncertain future with the hope of better times."

CHAPTER ELEVEN
LIVING THE DREAM

J ESSIE, DEAR DIARY, "IT HAS been fifteen years since I made an entry. I thought I had lost my diary, but thank God, he knew right where it was. Well, where do I begin? Louis and I have been living out our dream.

I am a Bible study group leader in our church. I teach women ages 18 to 30. Some are single and others are married with children. We do not follow a curriculum. Instead, we discuss topics we are interested in and see what the Bible says about them. Sometimes I assign portions of the chosen topic to group members to look up and present to the group. It is a lot of fun and we girls get to chat with each other along the way.

Can you believe it? I am 39 years old. Louis, my wonderful husband, is 40. The best part is that after 15 years, we are still in love. He adores me and I love him with all my heart.

Louis is now head of the detectives and the self-defense instructor to the entire police force. He teaches the officers the art of self-defense as an officer of the law. It is a completely different posture because of the threat of police abuse lawsuits.

I am writing this diary as a family keepsake. I have this feeling that folks a hundred years from now will enjoy reading it. They will know some of what life was about in my generation. Of course, this means I will have to talk about family, friends, weather, political life, and a lot more. Where do I begin? Maybe I should say, Dear future family.

As I think about the past 15 years, I must give God all the praise and glory. It was his grace that led me to Louis. It was his mercy that delivered me from harm. It was his blessings that prospered us. I am truly grateful.

I guess it is time to pick up the story where I left off fifteen years ago. My diary entries ended with my husband shooting my birth Mother who had just killed my aunt that raised me as her own child and my son, who killed my dad, his uncle, that we all thought died in WWII. Oh yeah, then there was my grandma that had a heart attack and died several days later. Finally, Louis and I were married and immediately orchestrated three funerals. It was then that I realized I was all alone.

As I struggled with what to do next. I remembered a scripture that said something to the effect, Faith Comes By Hearing and Hearing by The Word of God. So I opened my Bible and began to read, hoping God would speak to me in the scriptures and I would be strengthened in my faith.

I opened the Bible to 2 Corinthians 5:7. It says, "We walk by faith and not by sight." I knew it was the Holy Spirit telling me I was trying to use my natural eyes to see what to do next. Then he reminded me of Romans 8:28 that says, "God works all things together for good to those who fear (Reverence) God and are called according to his purposes."

These two scriptures helped me to understand that

God wanted me to walk by faith, knowing that he will work everything out for my good. I can rest and be at peace in my emotions because God is at work on my behalf. So, I put my trust in the Lord and waited for instruction as to my future.

It was not long after my "Word" from God that I received a letter in the mail. The letter, which was addressed to me, showed a return address of the Federal Bureau of Investigation, Washington, DC. The letter was a Federal Mandate. It ordered me to appear in Washington to discuss a matter of national security.

Why was I being summoned to appear before the FBI? What do I know about national security matters? This is amazing. Louis figured it might be something that Suzie was involved in before he shot her, and that since I was her twin, I might have information. I guess we will see what goes down."

CHAPTER TWELVE
THE FBI AND
MOREFAMILY SECRETS

L ouis, "I will go with you to Washington. You will need an advocate to protect your rights.

Jessie, Deare Diary" I am afraid but I do not believe I did anything wrong. This is crazy."

Louis, "We need to get started. Our meeting with the FBI is on Wednesday. That is only two days from now."

Jessie, "I'll get my things. We have tickets for American Airlines flight #43, leaving at 6:40 AM."

Dear Diary, "Soon we will sit before government officials. I am afraid. Help me, Lord, to get through this stressful time."

Bill Thomas (FBI Official)" Please have a seat. I will be with you in a moment. Tammy? Take this dispatch to the post office. It needs to be in Mexico City on Saturday. Be sure you mark it top secret and deliver it in person."

"Ok, now where were we? Oh yeah, I summoned you to Washington on a matter of national security. It is of utmost importance and we must maintain confidentiality. What I am about to tell you is top secret. You cannot discuss it with anyone, not even family. Here are the papers to sign before we get started. By signing them, you agree you will tell no one. If you do, we may put you in federal prison."

Bill Thomas continues, "Your mother's twin sister was a Nazi collaborator during WWII."

Jessie, "Are you referring to Mary or Suzie? They both claimed motherhood over me.?

Bill Thomas, "I am referring to Suzie, your birth mother. She went by many names over the years. We were tracking her movements right up to the time of her death on your farm.

Louis, "How does Jessie fit into this story? She never met her birth mother until she showed up one day with a crazy story about being her mother.

Bill Thomas, "As you may know, the Nazis stole the wealth of over 29 million people that went into the gas chambers plus the treasures of every country they conquered. Hitler hid this great wealth in many locations, one of which was Iowa, using your birth mother, their American collaborator. We believe that a vast amount of gold is hidden somewhere on your farm. We want you to search for it as part of your farming duties so as not to raise questions."

Louis, "What does Jessie get for all her effort?"

Bill Thomas, "How about the thank you from a grateful nation at a private dinner with the President of the United States?"

Jessie, "I don't think so. I did not vote for him, and I do not need a private dinner. If that is all you can offer, forget about it."

Bill Thomas, "Ok, what do you want? I will see what I can do.?

Jessie, "There must be billions stashed away somewhere on this farm. If I find it, I want a healthy finder's fee, say 10% of the total value. Plus, just for looking, I want no more taxes on my land or family income. I want state-of-the-art farm equipment that I can use for digging for gold, planting, and harvesting crops. It will have to look like I am a true farmer. I will need a new truck and a repair crew to make repairs to the farmhouse and outbuildings. I want FBI funded farm hands, at least four, to help with the growing and harvesting of crops. Finally, I will need $25,000 in cash for incidentals. What do you think, Louis? Is that enough?

Louis, "I think that will do the job. However, you should be allowed to add a few things later to your list if needed, say three more additions."

Jessie, "Ok, Mister Thomass, put all this in writing and we have a deal. Nothing will start until I have the signed agreement, the new truck, farm equipment, cash in the bank and workers."

Bill Thomas, "Alright! I will see what the US Government wants to do. Don't you think that is a bit much?

Jessie, "No Sir, I do not. If there is gold in them there hills, it has to be worth billions. Hey Louis, let's go back to Iowa and look around for hidden treasure."

Louis, I'll check on our return flight."

Bill Thomas, I will notify you as soon as I get an answer to your proposal."

(Jessie and Louis returned to Iowa and waited for an answer from the FBI. In the meantime, Louis started work repairing the pump that kept the water running to the farmhouse and property.)

Louis, "Hey Jessie, come here. I am in the pump house. I found something.

Jessie, "What is it, a gold bar?"

Louis, "No darling, it is a handwritten map, I think."

Jessie, "Let me look at it? Bring it into the light. No, silly, it ain't no map. It is a grocery list."

Louis, "No dear, look at the other side."

Jessie, Oh yeah, there are lines that connect fruit and vegetables in a pattern of sorts. Could this be a map?

Louis, "I think so. Let's take it into the house and look it over more closely.

(So Jessie and Louis spent the better part of the night trying to figure out a starting point and where the "X" was that marked the spot. They went from okra to carrots to apples to cornstalks and back again, passing the tomatoes each time.)

Jessie, "I just cannot figure this out. There is no key to what the fruit and vegetables stand for."

Louis, "Wait a minute. Where do we grow carrots? In the north field, right? Where do we grow apples? In the apple orchard, right? I got it. The gold is under the tomatoes."

Jessie, " All we have to do is plow up 10 acres of tomato plants. That should be fun.

Louis, "I pulled this hand written receipt off the list. It was attached. There is a date. It says June, 23rd 1928. I can hardly make it out, but that is the date."

Jessie, "That cannot be what we are looking for. Oh well, let's start dinner. Tomorrow is another day. If the

Lord wants us to find the Nazi gold, we will. He will guide us to the place where it is buried.

Jessie, Dear Diary, "This could be big. I am afraid that the government will not keep its word or criminals will steal it before we can collect. If it all works out, I will use the wealth to bless others less fortunate and sponsor some church activities." I wonder how much is there? It may not be on the farm at all."

Louis, "I do not want to get us all stressed out over a get rich quick possibility. I think we ought to relax, wait on the Lord and see what he will reveal to us. What do you think, Jessie?"

Jessie, "I must tell you. Last night I opened my Bible, and this just jumped off the page. It seemed to scream at me, saying, "The wealth of the sinner is laid up for the just." Proverbs 13:22. I think God wants us to know that he has kept this gold for us."

Louis, "However, remember that the Bible also says, ***"For where your treasure is, there will your heart be also."*** Matthew 6:21. We cannot put our hearts towards chasing treasure that might be at the end of the rainbow. God is our source, not Nazi gold. Doesn't the Bible also say, "for the love of money is the root of all evil.?" I Timothy 6:12 .

Jessie, "It is not having money that is evil, but the love of money, or covetousness, that leads to evil. You know that."

Louis, "Money brings power and power can corrupt. It is like living with a snake. One day, it will slither up to you and bite you in the butt."

Jessie, "Well, I am going to search for it and if I find

it, it will be all mine. I would not want to corrupt you. I will just sail away on my yacht while you look on."

Louis, "I don't think so. If you sail, I go with you."

Jessie, "Ok then, put your detective skills to work and find that treasure."

CHAPTER THIRTEEN
TREASURE! TRFEASURE! WHERE IS THE TREASURE?

(S o Jessie and Louis, sitting in the moonlight on their wrap-around porch, the same one where grandma used to sit, discuss various locations where there might be Nazi gold.)

Louis, "If there is gold, it was most likely melted down and transformed into bars. A single bar of gold can weigh from 20 to 40 lbs. each. That would be difficult to ship, move around or hide. Nazi gold bars were bigger than the normal ones. On the other hand, jewelry would most likely stay as it is to keep its value."

Jessie, "I bet Suzie dumped it in the lake that is in the south field." It is close to the tree line and easy to access. No one can see you come and go."

Louis, "We have no real clues. There are no tire tracks, no map, not anything. All we have is 40 acres to dig up and a farmhouse with outbuildings to tear apart. I think we should just forget the whole thing."

Jessie, "Not on your life. I will tear down and re-build if I have to. It must be here somewhere."

Joe, "Hi mom, what are you all up to? Can I help?"

Jessie, "No thanks. We are just looking around to see if anything needs repair."

Joe, "Oh yeah, this letter came in today's mail. It looks official."

Louis, "Give it to me. I handle all the official stuff.

(Joe goes off on his own and Louis reads the letter from Bill Thomas/FBI.)

"After our meeting a few weeks ago, I presented your proposal. Here is what they will do:

- $25,000 cash for incidentals.

- New top of the line truck of your choice.

- Four FBI farm hands for six months.

- New farm equipment as needed.

- FBI construction crew to tear down and rebuild as needed.

- 3% of total value instead of 10%

- An FBI supervisor to review and approve every action to keep cost to a minimum and actions germane to the project goal.

If you agree with these terms and conditions, please sign, date, and return this letter ASAP. Once we record your acceptance, we will notify you as to a starting date."

Louis continues, "Well dear, you got most of what you asked for."

Jessie, "I did not get the wavier on taxes, but I guess if we find the gold, that will not matter."

(So Jessie signed the document and sent it back as instructed. Three weeks later, Sam Freeman, the FBI supervisor, shows up at the farm with four FBI agents/ farm workers.)

Sam, "Good morning, we are here to help you find the Nazi gold. I'd like to sit down over coffee and discuss how we will start."

Jessie, "ok, come on in, gentlemen. I will put on a pot of coffee and clear the kitchen table so you have room for all your papers."

Sam, "I have the original building plans for this farmhouse. I want to start in the basement, then the attic, and then behind suspicious walls that might hide treasure."

Sam continues, "You two, check out the attic. Pull up the floorboards and see what is under them. The three of us will work in the basement. Remember, we are looking for jewelry, precious stones, and gold bars."

(So they dug up the basement and tore up the attic, looking for the pot of gold at the end of the rainbow. Hours went by until around three p.m. They made a gruesome discovery in the basement. Two human skeletons lay wrapped in fine linen sheets about three feet under the basement floor. There were two gold bars on top of the human remains. The Nazi swastika symbol marked both bars.)

Sam, "Hello, Louis? This is Sam, the FBI guy. You better get over there quickly. We found two bodies and two gold bars in the basement."

Louis, "Ok, I will bring the coroner with me. Close off the basement. It is now a crime scene."

Jessie, (Bringing coffee to the FBI men in the basement) "Oh my God", she screams and she drops the tray with hot coffee. What is this?

Sam, "Your husband is on his way. The basement is now off limits to everyone except law enforcement folks."

Jessie, "Two bodies and two gold bars, WOW! It looks like the treasure is on my property, after all."

Louis, arriving with the coroner, "Ok, this is now a Sherriff's' Department investigation."

Sam, "I do not agree. The FBI has the authority and will lead the way. Because the crime happened on your property and you are head of the Sheriff's detectives, I will allow you to do the preliminary discovery. The office responsible for national security matters will oversee the rest of the investigation."

Jessie Dear Diary, "I cannot believe someone buried two human bodies in my basement. Who were they? Is this the work of Suzie? It is just too much for me to handle right now. Thank God for Louis."

Coroner, "These bodies have been here a long time. I would say well over 100 years. If this was a murder, someone committed it in the 1800s."

Sam, the FBI agent, "Well, that clears that up."

Jessie, "But who are they? Are they my relatives? Is there a way of knowing?"

Louis, "What about the two bars of gold? How did they get put in with the skeletons from the past? Someone had to dig in this area to hide the gold but decided not to because of the bodies. But why then leave just two bars?

Jessie, Dear Diary, "I hate this not knowing. Every clue we find leads nowhere. God help us."

(So Jessie began to search family history records, hoping to find out who the two people were that are now lying in her basement. Several days passed, but she was successful.)

Jessie, "Hey guys, look what I found? Listen to the family history record. "A young married couple was found down by the lake. Indians killed them. We took the arrows out of them and buried them in the farmhouse's basement that was being built. We had no family graveyard and did not want to start one with strangers." I guess that solves our mystery."

Louis, "It does for the people, but not how the gold got there. The mystery still lingers."

Sam, "There is another problem that the hunt for Nazi gold brings. The Neo-Nazi thugs want it badly and will kill to get it. I am even now talking with the Fort Des Moines Army Base. about stationing soldiers on the farm to guard it from Nazi invasion."

Jessie, "What is Neo-Nazism?

Bill, "The official definition is…Neo-Nazism comprises the post-World War II militant, social, and political movements that seek to revive and reinstate Nazi ideology. Neo-Nazis employ their ideology to promote hatred and racial supremacy (often white supremacy), to attack racial and ethnic minorities, often antisemitism. They want the gold to fund their radical agenda. It would be better if you left the farm until this is all over."

Jessie, "Not on your life. I can shoot a gun and will

if I must. I want my share of the treasure and will stick around and see this through."

(Several days passed, and the FBI saw strangers prowling around the farm. Louis increased his deputy's watch, but that did not stop the prowlers. Then it happened. Suddenly, over 400 army soldiers filled the farm. They set up perimeters and guard post and tents and a command center. It was a full field operation. The cover story for being there was military field exercises. They were there to protect the search for gold and the FBI efforts.)

Sam, "These soldiers have a lot of weapons which are loaded with live ammo. Be alert and stay away from their encampments."

Joe, (Jessie's 25-year-old son), "Mom, what is going on? Why is the Army camping on our land?"

Jessie, "They are here to protect us from some bad people that are trying to find buried treasure that your aunt Suzie put here. You cannot tell anyone, not even your girlfriend. Promise me you will say nothing. If you do, I will go to prison because I signed a secret document that says my family must say nothing."

Joe, "Ok, I will be quiet. Can I watch?"

Jessie, "Sure, but know that the army guys are using live ammo. Stay out of their way."

Sam, (Addressing a work committee), "So far, we have dredged the lake, ripped up the farmhouse and outbuildings, including the barn. There is no other place to look."

Joe, "Excuse me sir, there is one other place. As a

kid, I played in a cave not too far from the edge of the tree line beyond the apple orchard. It could be there."

Sam, "Get the boys together, load up the trucks. We will check it out now while we still have plenty of daylight."

(While the FBI and Joe are off to find the cave, a group of 60 Neo-Nazis rush the farmhouse. They came with weapons and fired them as they ran. The army fired back and 15 Nazis lay dead in the barnyard. The rest of the Neo-Nazis scattered in all directions, or the army captured them.)

Louis, "We found the motherlode. It was in the cave along with a huge black bear." There were 400 bars of gold weighing 20 lbs. each. That means to calculate the total value, we need to multiply 400 bars X 20 lbs. or 8,000 lbs. of gold, times 16 oz or 128,000 ounces. X $38 per ounce, for a total value of $4,864,000. Hey Jessie? your 3% finder's fee will be $145,920. Not bad for a day's work."

Sam, "Don't forget the 400 bars that weighed 40 lbs. each. That is another 16,000 lbs. 256,000 ounces. That totals $9,728,000 A 3% deal is another $291,840. Jessie will get $437,760, and it is all tax free."

(So the Army and the FBI went their own ways, leaving Jessie, Louis, and Joe to ponder all that had happened on gramma's farm.)

Joe, "Hey Louis, what happened to the two gold bars that were found in the basement?"

Jessie, "I can answer that question. I put them in my bedroom closet wrapped up in a beach towel. I put them away for you, Joe. A wedding gift for when you get married."

Joe, "Thanks mom, but what if the FBI remembers and wants them back?

Jessie, "Then we will give them back. Otherwise, they stay hidden and safe with me. I will give you the equivalent value in cash."

Joe, "Let's see, there are two 20 lb. bars. That is 40 lbs. of gold X 16 ounces each, or 640 ounces at $38 per ounce. You owe me $23,040. That is a nice chunk of change."

CHAPTER FOURTEEN
MY HUSBAND AND ME

"I BEGAN JOURNALING IN THIS DIARY in 1957. I was 14 years old. It is now 1982. Twenty-five years have come and gone. It reminds me of a comment in the scriptures that says, "And It Came To Pass." So did the years in my life. Some years brought sorrow, hardship, and death. But there were happy times. It is the happy times that I want to record in my diary so future family can know that life in my generation was not so bad."

Jessie, Dear Diary, "My husband, Louis is a great man. He is 6'1" tall, around 180 lbs. and all muscle. He is an outdoors person who loves to hunt and fish. He was a good father to Joe as he was growing up and was attentive to me and our children."

"Children? yes Louis and I have four beautiful kids. There is Mary, age 14, Louis Jr., age 12, Johnny, age 9 and Jancy, age 5. They are doing great in school and go to church with us every Sunday. Mary likes politics and will one day run for some kind of government office. Junior is like his dad. He wants to be a guide for fishing and hunting enthusiasts. It is too soon for the other two kids. They have yet to decide."

"My girlfriend, Julie, says husbands are a dime a dozen. You cannot count on them and they are not loyal. That may be her experience, but that is not my reality. My husband is honest as the day is long. He is kind, trustworthy and has a great sense of humor. He makes me laugh. He puts me and our family first. He also loves the Lord and prays with me every day. He makes me feel like I am a queen, especially when I feel like a slave. We do not have a 50/50 relationship. It is more like 100/100. Both of us put all of ourselves into our marriage. Our belief is that God comes first, then family and then work."

"Our farm requires a lot of work and the apple orchard is sometimes overwhelming. However, Louis sees to it that we set aside one night a week for a date-night out. We may just go out to a pleasant restaurant or add a movie to the night or just be alone by the fireplace with popcorn and a card game. We might just sit on the antique swing on the front porch with a glass of ice tea, gaze at the stars, hold hands, and smooch. The important thing is to be together in a close romantic encounter that is pleasing to both of us."

"Yes, we argue a lot over a bunch of different things. But what makes it ok as we understand it is life kicking back at us and we do not have to blame each other for what goes on. Plus, we usually apply Ephesians 4:26 *"Be ye angry, and sin not: let not the sun go down upon your wrath:"* If we are mad or angry, we will stay up all night if necessary to resolve the conflict. We will not let the sun go down (Fall asleep) until we are friends again and even lovers. We see our relationship as us against the world and with God at our side, we can always find a way."

"Although we are two distinct personalities, we

seem to have merged into one. The more we are together, the more we think alike, like the same things, and seek the same goals in life. Sometimes I am not sure where Louis ends and I begin or I end and he begins. Sometimes, he can even finish my sentences when we are talking. It is as though I married myself. He is me in male form and I am him in female form. I guess that is what the Bible means when it says, *"Therefore shall a man leave his father and his mother, and shall cleave unto his wife: and they shall be one flesh."* Genesis 2:24. It sure seems to me that God wanted man to be male and female, joined by his love and Holy Spirit. I am pleased to report that we are fulfilling God's divine destiny for man on earth. It is a good feeling to know that Louis and I are in his will, doing what he wants and living in his grace."

"Our love has been tried and tested many times and is still thriving. Wars and rumors of wars have not separated us. An immoral society with free sex and lots of drugs has not deterred us. A poor economy and harsh weather have not kept us from being in love. We are the real thing and I hope we stay this way all the days of our life. My husband is wonderful and I love him."

CHAPTER FIFTEEN
LOUIS AND THE ORDEAL

"T HE BIBLE SAYS, *"MANY ARE THE AFFLICTIONS of the righteous: but the LORD deliver him out of them all."* I guess this scripture relates best as an example of my husband's ordeal. You know he is the head over the detective division of the county sheriffs. There are only three other deputies, but Louis is the boss. Well, crime was on the increase in our country. The drug dealers came looking for out-of-the way places to make their drugs, store them and sell them. They set up several locations and went after our school children. It was a terrible time. The local news was full of drug overdoses, murders, and prostitution. Our sleepy little community was ablaze with evil men and their drugs."

"Louis was always working overtime, chasing down suspects and criminals. He was making headway until one day several well-respected leaders accused him of being the kingpin for the drug cartel. However, the lie took hold and folks started to believe it. As a result, authorities charged him and sent him to jail to await trial. I bailed him out, but the entire community turned against us."

"The deputies under him supported him, but no one listened. They wanted to know where we got all the money that suddenly showed up in our bank accounts.

We could not disclose that information or we would violate our agreement with the government. Louis told them to trace back the deposit to its origin and they will see it was not from drugs."

"One of the two upstanding citizens got caught in a sting operation and turned state's evidence. That was the only thing that saved Louis. There was a trial, and the district attorney traced back the large deposits in our accounts, only to find it came from the treasury department of the United States. Despite being declared innocent of all charges, the community continued to believe the lie about Louis. Our church asked us to leave. Many of our friends backed away from us and our apple sales plummeted. Never-the-less, we went on, giving thanks to God for delivering us from the hand of the enemy."

"Louis is now free from the Sherriff's job. He took an early retirement. He now picks apples, plays chess with Johnny, and sips on homemade apple juice."

"This experience showed me several things:

- Some folks will not accept the truth, even when it is right in front of them.

- Other folks were looking for a reason to reject you because they were jealous.

- Yet others are really children of darkness in sheep's clothing, just waiting to spread lies and cause confusion.

- Loyal friends and associates ask for evidence and believe it when shown. They do not leave.

- The devil will use anyone who is not listening to

God against you to criticize, gossip, lie against truth, and create hostility. Beware of those that do not walk with God.

Louis and I took a long-needed vacation and went to Europe. We toured all the countries, sipped French wine, ate Italian spaghetti, and drank beer in an English pub. It was a refreshing time."

"Louis's ordeal went on for several years. We had to face the gossipers, stand against the rejection, and ignore the tension but, finally it all calmed down. Those who wanted to be our friends were, and those who stayed critical drifted into the sunset. Life went back to normal."

CHAPTER SIXTEEN
LIVING AS A CHRFISTIAN IN AN UPSIDEDON WORLD

J ESSIE, "I GUESS THIS DIARY will become the life and times of Jessie and Louis. Folks 100 years from now will read all about us. That is why I am making sure that I tell it like it was, as I experienced it, and not hide the truth. I realize that what I say is based on my personal values and perspectives. However, as a Christian, I want to reveal Jesus in our lives and how it was to follow him in an upside-down world.

"Upside down is the reverse of right side up. When I was growing up, the world seemed to me to be where morality ruled the day and society looked down on those that were immoral. But now that I am getting older, my view of society and the world flipped to being immoral as the normal way of living and morality as the place not to be. I see most folks saying that using illegal drugs is ok, sex before marriage is cool, there are no absolutes anymore, God is dead, man is alive unto himself, there is no heaven or hell and no respect for women or conservative thinking."

"The news reports only the bad things that happen or attack those that stand for godly values. Christians are ridiculed for their faith and portrayed as being out of touch with reality."

"Years ago, being a pastor was a position that everyone admired. Young men would express their desire to be a pastor more than any other vocation. Times have sure changed and not for the better"

"If you are living 100 years from now, beware of false prophets, teachers, doctrines, and religions. What is happening in my generation are signs of what Jesus said in Matthew chapter 24 about life before the end of the world. If society persecutes Christians now, they will also persecute them in your generation."

"The way to overcome these evildoers is to trust in Jesus, follow his teachings and let your light shine before this upside-down world. You will be like a lighthouse in the dark of night. You may be the only Bible folks will ever read. Live out your Christian faith. Let God be God in you and let him direct you in all that you do."

"My generation is full of antichrists. They are folks that deny Jesus ever came to earth in human form. They say he is not the God-Man (God dwelling in Jesus) and that he did not die for the sins of all mankind. The fact is, he died for the sins of the entire world. John 3:16 records Jesus saying just that. He is the only way to God, the Father. These folks are false Christians, fakes, foolish self-absorbed individuals. If they are in your generation, reject them and stay away from their teachings."

Read your Bible and gather key scriptures. They can be hooks to hang your faith on. Here are a few that I found and use every day. They will help you live your Christian life in an upside-down, crazy world.

- Follow the 10-commandments.
- Bless and forgive them that despitefully use you.
- Walk by faith and not by sight.
- Walk in the Spirit and you will not fulfill the lust of the flesh.
- Submit yourself unto God, resist the devil, and he will flee from you.
- Trust in the Lord with all your heart and lean not unto your own understandings.
- Cast down all imaginations and everything that exalts itself above the knowledge of God.
- Beware of false prophets and fake Christians that deny that Jesus is not God in the flesh.
- Let your light so shine among men that they will see your good works and glorify God.
- Let the peace of God rule in your heart.
- Guard your heart, for out of it flows the issues of life.
- Cast your burdens upon the Lord for he cares for you.

I may not have quoted these scripture references exactly, but you get the point, right?

"Louis and I will go on living out our Christian life, being blessed by our Creator and blessing him with our reverence and thankfulness."

CHAPTER SEVENTEEN
TIME OVER TIME

JESSIE, DEAR DIARY, "TODAY IS July 3ʳᵈ 2021. It has been almost 40 years since I last recorded anything. Until now, I just didn't see the point. But then I thought it might be nice to continue for all my grandkids and their kids. I am pushing 80 and most likely will pass on into the arms of Jesus soon. Now I am all alone. I live in my memories because old ladies like me do not fit into the modern generation. All that was mine has faded away: my husband, Louis, my horse, Domino, my dog, Meatball, most of my high school friends and even the music of my times has given way to new and strange sounds.

I miss Louis. He passed about 20 years ago from cancer. He was my life and heartthrob. He kept me going and made my life worthwhile. Now, it is just me waiting to exhale.

Over the last 40 years, I watched my family grow up and become what they wanted to be. Johnny, Joe's son, became a doctor and saved many lives as a brain surgeon. He had three kids who are now all married with their own kids.

Joe is a grandpa. He sticks close to the farm and watches over all the family. He is a good man. What can I say about my life during the last years? It feels

"

like I was wandering in the wilderness of life looking for the promised land.

I witnessed wars, new inventions, race riots, rising crime, human trafficking, an explosion of illegal drugs, political unrest, woman's liberation protest, gay rights demonstrations, a transgender movement, movie star suicides, a big falling away from faith in the Christian community, the legalization of abortion, the elections of several presidents, the increase in the price of gas, groceries, housing and taxes, the persecution of Christians, and a lot more.

I also saw, firsthand, the power of God in my life that kept me from harm and guided me through all the difficulties. I saw healings, miracles, answered prayers, and deliverances from the many snares of the devil. I received multiple blessings from the Lord, both financial and spiritual.

I am still standing in my faith and proclaiming the good news of Jesus, the Christ of God. Though my trials have been many, God has delivered me from them all. I can say, without any doubts, that I am ready to meet my maker, face to face.

CHAPTER EIGHTEEN
TIMES PAST BUT NOT FORGOTTEN

"OVER THE PAST 40 YEARS, I have experienced several significant events that are worth discussing, even though I am talking to myself as I write in my tattered and worn journal. The first is a dream I had about 25 years ago. I can remember it as if it had happened last night. It was a Saturday night. The wind was blowing hard, and it was raining. I retired for the night a little after midnight and I quickly dropped off to sleep. The wind and rain were soothing and brought me a sense of peace."

I DREAMED A DREAM

"As I entered a deep sleep, I began to dream. However, it felt more like I was awake, and watching future events unfold. I saw them projected onto a gigantic screen that seemed to float in the clouds. These were the future events of my life. I knew that because I was the subject of the dream and the events that unfolded had not yet happened."

"I saw a bumper crop of corn, potatoes, and apples all in one year. I saw a tornado tearing apart our barn and destroying several trees. I saw horses and other farm animals running away from a wildfire that threatened homes on our farm. I saw six great grandkids being born of family members. I saw a plane crash in the distant mountains." They were like visions, yet I know I was dreaming."

"Then I saw an angel with wings flying across the heavens. He appeared to be about 9-feet tall and was dressed in a white robe. He looked over at me as he flew by and smiled. He had a trumpet in his hand."

"Finally, It was my beloved husband, Louis, my mother, Mary, and my grandma Elizabeth walking together along a narrow road. The street sign that said, "This is the highway called Holiness that leads to the throne of God." Suddenly, they stopped walking and beckoned for me to come and join them. I cried because I could not join them. But then a voice echoed in my mind with a single word, Soon. Repeatedly, I heard the word "Soon" echoing in my mind."

"Some of what I dreamed about has already come to pass. There was a tornado back about five years ago, and it destroyed parts of our barn. It also tore away several trees. Five of the six great grandkids were born just last year. I am waiting for the rest to happen. I know all will come to pass because the angel smiled upon me and the voice from heaven said, "Soon.""

"There are more significant events hidden in my past. Once upon a time, aliens abducted me, but not really. I just wanted to see if you were listening."

MORE NAZI GOLD

"Joe and I went back to the cave where we found the gold, thinking that there might be more. The FBI just saw and took what was visible. They did not explore the rest of the cave. We wanted to look further back and guess what? There were more gold bars. We found another 500, 40 lb. bars, tucked away in an offshoot of the cave that led to an opening far away from where we entered. We resolved the gold situation years ago. Now it is in our face again. Well, it was 10 years ago. It was 2002 when we discovered the extra gold. The value then was $310 per troy ounce. That is 20,000 ounces X $310 each or $6,200,000. My finder's fee is 3% or $186,000. We called the FBI, but Sam was no longer there and we could find no that wanted to talk to us. So, the Nazi gold remains hidden in a new location on our property for future generations to find. Joe is working on a treasure map."

THE VOICE FROM ABOVE

"There was a voice that came from heaven in my dream. At least I think it was from heaven. I believe it was because it said, "SOON." What did "soon" mean?" What was going to happen, "soon"? I have pondered this "soon" thing for years. The best I can figure is that the voice was referring to the return of Jesus for his church. I hope that is so because I really want to experience being caught up in the air with other believers to meet the Lord. I can imagine what that would be like. On the way up, I'll be screaming, "I Can fly! "I Can Fly!" Then I will join all the other saints that came with him in a glorious song of praise. He is coming with his saints, you know? That means I will see Louis, Grandma and Mary riding on heavenly horses. Maybe Domino will be there for me to ride on the way back to glory…and Meatball jumping in my arms with lots of kisses. It will be a great time and I look forward to it, if that is what the voice meant when it said, "soon" I hope so."

THE MIRACLE OF DESTINY

"I remember one other thing. I call it the miracle of destiny. Sixty-five years ago, I had a friend. Her name was Julie. She was thirteen years old. She was just as wild as me. We skipped school together; ran with the gangbangers; smoked dope, beat up other girls for no reason; and hated just about everyone and everything. We felt that life owed us stuff. We were not sure what stuff but, life owed it to us. She was a foster child. Her mother was dead and her father was in prison for grand theft auto.

"Long story short, Julie ended up in the state reform school for wayward girls. I never saw her again until about ten years ago. We both started life in Miami, but Julie found her way to my front door as a representative of the *Jesus For Iowa Girls' Association*. She did not know who she was speaking to, just looking for a place to bring wayward girls to summer camp and rehabilitation. I invited her in and we shared a pot of tea and some homemade apple pie. During our conversation, she mentioned she was a wayward girl that went through reform school and how terrible it was. It was then that I told her about my childhood friend from Miami and what happened to her. We both realized that she was my long-lost friend."

"The miracle of destiny was that God had miraculously led her to me. She was destined to find me and we were destined to labor together in His name."

"Most folks do not believe in divine destiny, but I do. The Bible tells us this. Psalm 37:23 says, *"The steps of a good man are ordered by the LORD: and he delights in his way."* The verse is a reminder that God is in control of our lives and that we should trust Him to guide us in the right direction. The miracle is that God wanted me to see all the great work He has done in Julie's heart. She too started out on the wrong foot but God got ahold of her and led her to a better life where she now helps other girls find their way."

"We set up a summer camp. I funded it and even gave Julie a job so she could remain on the farm and be free to plan and execute summer camps. She is now part of our extended family. She has been living and working on the farm for the last 15-years."

As I mentioned before, I am wanting to exhale. I am sure to meet Jesus, either at my death or his coming, which is soon.

CONCLUSION

Every book should have a conclusion. I guess this one is no different. But what do I say? This is a fictional story with fictitious characters doing things that are a projection of the author's imagination. The value of such a fictional story is that you, the reader, can experience different life situations and see how they relate to your life. God loves you and wants to bless you.

In the story, we looked at teen and adult suicide; abortion; loss of a love one; deception; forgiveness; the concept of God; the reality of sin and its consequences; death and beyond; reasons for living; the abundant life, Christian values, good house rules for teens. why we exist; how to be born again, and several other life issues.

If there is a central theme from which we can see truth and apply knowledge, it would be the knowledge of God and his ability to work every situation out for good to those that reverence him and are called in accordance with his purposes.

ABOUT THE AUTHOR

Rev. Marinelli is an ordained minister, He has formed and been pastor of one church in Wisconsin and was the pastor of another in Alabama. He has also been a youth minister and evangelism director over the years.

Rev. Marinelli has authored over 30-books that can be viewed on his website:

www.marrinellichristianbooks.com

John is an accomplished Christian poet. He also dabbles in songwriting and writing one act Christian plays. He is the Vice President of Have A Heart For Companion Animals, Inc., a "No Kill" animal welfare organization. He volunteers his time promoting fundraising events for www.haveaheartusa.org.

Rev. Marinelli is now retired from the sales and marketing arena after spending over 40 years in business-to-business and non-profit marketing. He enjoys writing Christian themed books, playing chess, singing karaoke and a retired lifestyle in sunny Florida

For More Info eMail Contact:

johnmarinelli@embarqmail.com

SELECTED CHRISTIAN POETRY BY JOHN MARINELLI, THE AUTHOR

"I AM" THERE

"I AM" There,
At the end of your broken dreams,
Before the sun rises over your day,
Prior to those tear-filled streams.

"I AM" There,
Down that road of despair,
When all appears to be lost,
And no one seems to care.

"I AM" There,
Over all of life's twists and turns,
When tomorrow is all but gone,
And when you are full of concerns.

"I AM" There,
Sayeth the Lord of Host,
To bring you hope and peace,
And the power of my Holy Ghost.

"I AM" There,
To be sure you make it through,
In the midst of every trial,
To bless your life and deliver you.

"I Am" There

"All power is given unto me in heaven and earth. Go ye therefore and teach all nations, baptizing them in the name of the Father, and of the Son, and of the Holy Ghost: Teaching them to observe all things, whatsoever I have commanded you: and lo, I am with you always, even unto the end of the world." Mathew 28:18-20

The Lord is with us always. He never leaves our side, even when we leave His. In every situation, He is there. It's time to count on His presence and trust in His grace.

GUARDIAN ANGEL

The Angel of the Lord
Comes with a mighty army,
To fight the enemies of God.

Then he opens our eyes
That we might see the battle
And walk where angels trod.

Our guardian angels
Beholds the very face of God,
Standing there on our behalf.

Our guardian angels
Are ready with God's power,
To quiet evil's awful wrath.

"Take heed that ye despise not one of these little ones; for I say unto you, That in heaven, there angels do always behold the face of my Father, which is in heaven" Mathew 18:10

As God's children, we have guardian angels that watch over us and report back to God. They are ministering spirits especially placed in service to help the saints on their way to glory.

THE ANGEL'S CAMP

The angel of the Lord
Sets up his camp
Around those that reverence God.

Imagine being there
In the midst of
Where angels trod.

What a joy it is
To know God's protection
And to be in the angel's camp.

It is there that God's children
Are delivered from evil's woe
And led by heaven's lamp.

"The angel of the Lord encamps round about them that fear Him, and delivers them" Psalm 34:7

Deliverance come through reverence and respect for God and a belief that He will be there with His angels to help you in times of trouble.

ALL CREATION WAITS

A blue-gray sky
Winks at the dawn,
As the morning light
Sings its glorious song.

Life is flourishing everywhere,
Unaware of what's in store.
The sounds of spring beckons,
In a silent and peaceful roar.

Time marches onward,
Towards the brink of day,
As all of creation waits
For God's children to pray.

It's time to stand up and be counted as a child of God. It's time to pray for peace and deliverance. Creation is waiting.

DON'T WORRY

Don't worry about tomorrow.
You did that yesterday.
Go on with your life
And remember always to pray.

Ask and it shall be given to you,
But this great truth you already know.
Rejoice and be happy, why? Because…
Your harvest comes from what you sow.

I will say it again and even more,
Until it becomes very very clear.
Tomorrow will take care of itself,
But worry is another word for fear.

Now here's what I want you to do.
Trust in the Lord and be of good cheer.
Drop the worry from your vocabulary
And cast out that demon of fear.

Worry is a sin so stop it. Be of good cheer. It's all up to you. Life is too short to spend it worrying.

ARM'S LENGTH

I hold the world at arm's length,
That its choices do not interfere.
While it does its own thing,
I watch and wait over here.

My steps must not go that way,
For it's not where I need to be.
The Lord has shown me the path,
That will lead me to my destiny.

The call to follow sin is strong
And pulls at me now and then.
But I know that way
Is full of sorrow and sin.

I must move on in life
Beyond their beckoning call.
It's the right thing to do,
So I do not stumble or fall.

I will not be swayed or misled
By family, friends or business deal.
Their secret thoughts are not mine,
To consider, to admire or feel.

So I keep the world at "Arm's Length"
As I journey through this life.
My faith in Jesus keeps me strong,
As I walk in His glorious light.

Arm's length is a good policy. Be sure you stay in the Lord and close to Him. It's the only way to keep sane in such a crazy world.

CLUTTER

Clutter keeps the mind confused,
As images dance through the night.
Lost among those unimportant thoughts,
Are the dreams that once shined bright.

An endless parade of fear and doubt,
Crowds the mind to destroy our day.
Ever soaring on the wings of the soul,
Until it has formed an evil array.

But clutter is by one's choice,
Of those who dance to its beat.
Better to face imaginations' due
Than to fall into utter defeat.

Set up a filter that keeps out unnecessary thoughts. A good practice is to go by the still waters in your mind and rest there until the flow of life situations becomes manageable.

I FIND MYSELF IN GOD

I find myself in God.
He is my "everything"
I know that He is Lord,
My Life, my Hope, and King.

I find myself in God,
Not the ways of sin.
Nor do I look to others,
To know who I really am.

I find myself in God,
To whom I bow on bended knee.
He alone is my joy and strength
And where I want to be.

You cannot really know yourself unless you first know God. He created you in His images and until you discover Him, you will never find yourself.

THE ANGELS CRY "HOLY,"

The Angels cry "Holy,"
While sorrow fills the land.
For God's Judgment Day,
Is to come upon every man.

The Angels cry "Holy,"
While mankind goes astray,
Rejecting the love of God,
To follow his own precarious way.

The Angels cry "Holy,"
Knowing the terror of the Lord,
When all who dwell in sin,
Will suddenly be destroyed.

The Angels cry "Holy,"
Waiting for all things new,
Born of the Holy Spirit,
When God's Judgment is through.

The Angels cry "Holy,"
"Holy is the Lamb,"
Waiting for the children of God,
To join "The Great I AM"

Heaven is waiting for us to join our Savior. What a great day that will be. Are you ready? I am.

REST MY CHILD

Take your peace and be restored
Then put your faith in Jesus, the Lord
He has provided, your mouth to feed.
From the beginning, He knew your need.

Do not worry, fret or even fear,
for, my child, He is always near.
To bless your soul with love and grace,
To be with you, face to face.

Come, my child, near to His throne.
Do not allow your faith to roam.
For those who will not believe,
Can never find rest in times of need.

His word shall see you through.
His grace He freely gives to you.
That you should rest, your soul to keep,
Forever delivered from unbelief.

Go ahead, rest in the Lord. I dare you. It may be scary
at first but it sure feels good when you get use to it.

WINNING THE BATTLE

We must use the Word of God
To calm emotions that fray.
For the enemy never sleeps,
Until he has led us astray.

So when your emotions overflow
With feelings like depression and fear.
Know this! If you dwell in that place,
You invite the enemy to draw near.

When your emotions rage
With fiery darts aglow,
Stand in the power of the Lord,
Against its awful woe.

And if you get confused
And lost in the storm,
Put your thoughts on trial,
Rejecting all but heaven born.

You can win the battle
That rages within your soul.
By casting down imaginations,
And breaking Satan's hold.

Remember to focus on Jesus,
Holding the world at arm's length.
Lift up your head above the trial,
And the Lord will give you strength.

"For the weapons of our warfare are not carnal but mighty, through God, to the pulling down of strongholds: casting down imaginations and every high thing that exalts itself against the knowledge of God, and bringing into captivity every thought to the obedience of Christ." II Corinthians 10:3-5 The battle is in our minds and we win by putting our thoughts on trial and casting out all that oppose the knowledge of God. This is true victory.

LITTLE PRISONS

Little prisons await the man with a lustful soul.
Bars of selfishness and pride cre-
ate dungeons of icy cold.

Prisons of shame and jealousy fill
the heart with utter despair.
Bars that separate from God
and those that really care.

Stand back! While the doors are tightly closed;
Taking away your life, to wither as a dying rose.

Beware of those little prisons that trap the lustful soul.
Keep yourself free from sin through
faith in the Christ of old.

Little prisons need not to be your fate.
It is your choice, Spirit or flesh to date.

"O Foolish Galatians, who hath bewitched you, that ye should not obey the truth, before whose eyes Jesus Christ hath been, evidently set forth, crucified among you? Are you so foolish? Having begun in the Spirit, are you now made perfect in the flesh?

We should always seek to dwell in the Spirit, that we would not emulate the deeds of the flesh. When we fall short, we create "little prisons" that keep us in confusion and away from the blessing of God. It's time to walk in the Spirit and break the prisons that so easily beset us

THE WRESTLING MATCH

We wrestle not with flesh and blood,
For man is not our enemy.
Instead, we fight demons in the spirit
That seek to steal our destiny.

But our weapons are not earthly,
Like tanks, guns or bombs.
Instead, we "Plead The Blood"
And shout our victory songs.

So do not wrestle with humanity
Even though evil is there.
Go after Satan, the real enemy
And strip his kingdom bare.

"For though we walk in the flesh, we do not war after the flesh: for the weapons of our warfare are not carnal but mighty, through God, to the pulling down of strongholds; casting down imaginations and every high thing that exalts itself above the knowledge of God, and bring into captivity, every thought to the obedience of Christ." II Corinthians 10: 3-6

Don't fight with other people. Just go about your own business, counting on God to be the avenger. He is the one that holds all the power and strength. If we fight in the flesh, we can fall to strongholds and demons. But standing up in the Spirit and using the name of Jesus, applying the knowledge of God in the situation and casting down every ungodly imagination, will always lead us to victory.

OH' THE BLOOD

Oh, the blood of Jesus
That washed away my sin.
What a great blessing
To have God as my friend.

This one thing I know for sure,
That when I confess my sin,
His cleansing blood will flow,
And I can walk again with Him.

Oh, the blood of Jesus,
How great a sacrifice for me.
For it was the blood of the Lamb
That healed my soul and set me free.

"If we confess our sins, he is faithful and just to forgive us our sins and to cleanse us from all unrighteousness." I John 1:9

It is the blood of Jesus that is the cleansing agent in forgiveness, acceptance by God and salvation of the soul. Without His blood, there would be no payment for sin. Saint John, in chapter three, says that the wages for sin is death. Jesus paid the price so we could go free to serve God, the Father.

ONE MAN

It was by one man, Adam,
That the world fell into sin.
He chose to disobey God's word
And lost God's Spirit within.

No more walks with God
Through the garden of God's grace.
No more close up and personal
To walk along and talk, face to face.

One man, Adam, gave up
The very nature of God.
Never again to stroll along
Where angels once trod.

Evil now flows through his blood
Where only righteousness was before.
He gave up the Spirit of life
To open up death's awful door.

But one Man, Jesus, came from God
To seek and to save that which was lost.
The life of God in man, once again,
Because He paid sin's incredible cost.

"Therefore, as by one man, sin entered into the world, and death by sin; and so death passed upon all men, for that all have sinned. For as by one man's disobedience, many were made sinners, so by the obedience of one, many shall be made righteous." Romans 5:12 & 19

Adam fell and lost the Spirit of God inside of him because of his disobedience; But Jesus obeyed, did not fall and restored what Adam lost. All die in Adam because of sin but all who believe in Jesus shall live in Christ because of His righteousness.

IN THE FULLNESS OF TIME

In the fullness of time,
Jesus came, made of a woman.
Our Heavenly Father sent Him
Because our adoption was at hand.

He was born under the law,
So He might redeem us from it,
And to receive adoption as sons,
Being children of God, we sit.

We who God made His children,
Have the Spirit of His Son,
Deep within our heart of hearts,
So we can finally become one.

"But when the fullness of time was come, God sent forth his son, made of a woman, made under the law, to redeem them that were under the law, that we might receive the adoption of sons. And because we are sons, God has sent forth the spirit of his son into our hearts, crying, Abba, Father." Galatians 4:4-6

We are the adopted sons of God. We, like no other, have the indwelling presence of the Spirit of His Son, who cries out unto God the Father. If your spirit is not crying out to God, you may want to find out why?

FRAGILE FLOWER RED

As a flower in earthen sod,
I bloom for thee, oh God.
To blossom with the turn of spring;
To be to you, a beautiful thing.

I lift my Fragile Flower Red
Upward from my earthen bed;
To draw light from God above,
Strength and peace and joy and love.

As a flower, I bloom for thee
That passersby may stop and see.
Your fragrance and beauty I am,
Flowered in grace as a man.

As a flower in earthen sod,
I bloom for thee, oh God.
Upward, I lift my head,
As a Fragile Flower Red.

"Be not conformed to this world, but be ye transformed, by the renewing of your mind, that ye may prove what is that good and acceptable and perfect will of God."

When we look to God as our source, we blossom,

much like a flower that draws light from the sun. When we blossom, like a flower, we display the glory and beauty of our creator to all who care to stop and look. This is our divine providence.